# PEOPLE & ORGANISATIONS

*An analytical and evaluative approach to business studies*

**Malcolm Surridge**

Hodder & Stoughton

A MEMBER OF THE HODDER HEADLINE GROUP

# Acknowledgements

In loving memory of Bennice Surridge

Even though one person's name may appear on the cover of a book, it is in fact the result of the work of a team of people. This book is no exception. Andrew Gillespie demonstrated his creativity by developing the idea for this series of books and edited this volume, improving it in many ways. I am indebted to him for his constructive advice. Llinos Edwards and Melanie Hall at Hodder and Stoughton have performed miracles in producing the book in a remarkably short space of time. David Chell has provided me with numerous materials, which have enriched the text and saved many hours of research. As always, those who make the greatest contribution are those who are closest to you. Jackie has provided constant (and good humoured) support throughout this project, providing further evidence that teamwork is highly productive!

The author and publisher would like to thank the following for permission to reproduce copyright text material:

Andrew Bibby, p. 11; *Financial Times*, pp. 15, 19, 42; ONS, pp. 12, 125; The European Commission, pp. 13, 14; *The Guardian*, p. 11; *The Independent*, p. 42.

Orders: please contact Bookpoint Ltd, 78 Milton Park, Abingdon, Oxon OX14 4TD. Telephone: (44) 01235 827720, Fax: (44) 01235 400454. Lines are open from 9.00 – 6.00, Monday to Saturday, with a 24 hour message answering service. Email address: orders@bookpoint.co.uk

*British Library Cataloguing in Publication Data*
A catalogue record for this title is available from The British Library

ISBN 0 340 77231X

First published 2000
Impression number 10 9 8 7 6 5 4 3 2
Year 2005 2004 2003 2002 2001



Cover illustration by Jon H. Hamilton
Typeset by Fakenham Photosetting Ltd, Fakenham, Norfolk
Printed in Great Britain for Hodder & Stoughton Educational, a division of Hodder Headline Plc, 338 Euston Road, London NW1 3BH by J. W. Arrowsmith, Bristol.

# Contents

If you have any comments on this book or suggestions for future editions, the Series Editor would be pleased to hear from you on: **gillsp@hotmail.com**

# General introduction

This series of six books is designed specifically to develop the higher levels of skill needed for exam success and, at the same time, to provide you with a critical and detailed insight into the subject as a whole. The books are written by a team of highly experienced examiners and authors to provide you with the information and approach to achieve the best results. Whereas a traditional textbook tends to provide an explanation of topics, this series concentrates on developing ideas in a more analytical manner. When considering a topic such as human resource management, for example, the book will focus on issues such as:

- How does human resource management differ from personnel management?
- How useful is human resource management?
- To what extent can human resource management improve a firm's performance?
- Why do some firms reject the human resource management approach?

The whole approach of the series is intended to develop a questioning and evaluative understanding of business issues. The emphasis is on why certain factors are important, rather than merely describing what they are. Reading these books will provide you with new insights into topics and help you to develop a critical view of the issues involved in the different areas of the subject.

This particular book critically examines the management of people. It includes the following areas:

- leadership and management styles
- motivation, teamworking and empowerment
- organisational structure and culture
- communication in business
- human resource management.

Throughout the text we provide up-to-date examples of business behaviour in the form of **fact files** and **numerical investigations**. There are also numerous **progress checks** in each chapter to help you to review your understanding of the topics you have covered so far. Each chapter includes sample exam questions, students' answers (including marks awarded and marker's comments) and advice on how to answer specific types of question in the exam. We also provide a chapter which is designed to help you interpret and analyse numerical data from this syllabus area. Answers to the end of section questions are located in the *Teacher's Handbook* which accompanies the series.

Chapter 9 provides information on how the business concepts covered in the book are usually assessed in examinations and focuses on the key underlying issues in each topic; this will be invaluable when it comes to preparing for your exams.

Chapter 8 focuses on the most recent issues in this area of the syllabus to make sure you are completely up-to-date in your understanding and to provide you with the latest ideas to include in your answers.

Not only will this book provide you with a thorough understanding of the people and organisational structures to firms, it will also help you develop the approach you need to achieve top grades. It is an invaluable resource for students who want to achieve exam success.

# *The 'levels of response' approach to marking*

In A Level Business Studies candidates are assessed by their ability to demonstrate certain key skills. A student's final grade will depend on the extent to which he or she has shown the ability to analyse points, structure ideas and come to a reasoned conclusion. An A grade candidate is someone who demonstrates these skills consistently, whereas a C grade candidate shows them intermittently. To do well at A Level, students not only have to know the issues involved in each topic area, they also have to be able to develop their ideas. It is very important, therefore, that candidates provide some depth to their answers, rather than leaving many ideas undeveloped. In most cases students do better by analysing a few key points in their answers, rather than by listing many different ideas. Unfortunately, many students find it difficult to expand on their initial points; although they often demonstrate a good knowledge of the issues involved, they do not necessarily find it easy to explore these ideas further. The aim of this series of books is specifically to help you develop your ideas in more depth, which will enable you to do better in the exam.

The basic approach to assessment at A Level is the same for all the examination boards and is known as 'levels of response' marking. In its simplest form this means that the mark you get depends on the skill you have demonstrated. The higher the skill shown in your answer the higher your final mark.

There are four main levels of skill assessed at A Level. These are:

- synthesis and evaluation (the highest level skill)
- analysis
- explanation
- identification. (the lowest level)

As you can see the 'identification' of relevant factors is the lowest level skill. This means that listing ideas will not in itself achieve a high grade. What is important is that you explain these points (i.e. show what they mean), analyse them (i.e. show why they are significant) and evaluate them (i.e weigh up their relative importance).

In a typical question worth 9 marks, the mark scheme may look something like this:

candidate *evaluates* relevant factors 9–7 marks

candidate *analyses* relevant factors 6–5 marks

candidate *explains* relevant factors 4–3 marks

candidate *identifies* relevant factors 2–1 marks.

As you can see, a candidate who simply identifies factors can only achieve a maximum score of 2 out of 9. Regardless of how many different points he or she makes, if all the student has done is to list ideas they cannot get more than 2 marks in total. To move up the levels and gain more marks candidates need to demonstrate the higher level skills. Unfortunately, most textbooks spend so much time explaining ideas that they cannot do much to help develop the ability to analyse and evaluate. This series focuses throughout on these higher level skills to help you move up the levels of response in the exam and maximise your grade.

Imagine you were faced with a question which asked you to 'Discuss the factors which might increase employees' motivation'. A good answer would identify a few relevant factors, explain what is meant by them, develop their impact and then discuss their importance. For example:

'Employees may be motivated by greater authority. This might meet their higher level needs such as ego needs or self-actualisation needs. The firm may offer individuals the opportunity to use their own initiative, to organise their own project or to deal with customers directly. Alternatively, an employee may be motivated by working in a team, by having contact with other employees, by a listening management style or even by social events. These approaches might meet employees' social needs. However, what actually motivates employees depends on their particular needs, the present situation and the context of the situation. For example, greater authority without suitable rewards or in the context of poor working conditions, low pay and bad industrial relations may not motivate.'

This a strong answer which takes a couple of points and develops them in some depth. For comparison, consider this answer:

'Better pay, more authority, delegation, a bigger office, respect and feedback.'

This answer has many ideas but all of them are left undeveloped and so it is a much weaker answer.

More recent mark schemes adopt a slightly different approach in which content, application, analysis and evaluation are each given a mark, as in the example below. As you can see in this case (which is the mark scheme for an essay) you can gain up to 8 marks for content, 8 marks for application, 8 for analysis and 16 for evaluation. Within each category the levels approach is used so that strong evaluation can be awarded up to 16 marks, whereas more limited evaluation may only get 2 or 3 marks. The basic principles of this scheme are similar to the original levels of response model; certainly the message to candidates is clear: the higher marks require analysis and evaluation; the best marks require good analysis and evaluation! A content laden answer would only get a maximum of 8 marks.

| SKILL | CONTENT | APPLICATION | ANALYSIS | EVALUATION |
|---|---|---|---|---|
| Maximum number of marks | 8 marks | 8 marks | 8 marks | 16 marks |
| Level of response | 8–5 marks<br>Three or more relevant factors identified | 8–6 marks<br>Full explanation of factors | 8–6 marks<br>Full analysis using theory appropriately and accurately | 16–11 marks<br>Mature judgement shown in arguments and conclusions |
| | 4–3 marks<br>Two relevant factors identified | 5–3 marks<br>Some explanation of two or more factors | 5–3 marks<br>Analysis with some use of relevant theory | 10–5 marks<br>Judgement shown in arguments and/or conclusions |
| | 2–1 marks<br>One relevant factor identified | 2–1 marks<br>Some explanation of one factor | 2–1 marks<br>Limited analysis of question | 4–1 marks<br>Some judgement shown in text or conclusions |
| | 0 marks<br>No knowledge shown | 0 marks<br>No application or explanation | 0 marks<br>No analysis present | 0 marks<br>No judgement shown |

**Table 1.1** Example mark scheme

The key to success in examinations is to consistently demonstrate the ability to analyse and evaluate – this involves exploring a few of the points you have made. All of the books in this series take an approach which should develop your critical ability and make it easier for you to discuss your ideas in more depth.

# *The higher level skills*

## What is analysis?

To analyse a point you need to show why it *matters*. Why is it relevant to the question? Why is it important? Having made a point and explained what it actually means, you need to discuss its significance either by examining what caused it or by exploring its effect on the business. This is illustrated below.

Question: *Analyse the possible causes of poor communication within a firm.*

Answer: Poor communication may be due to there being too many levels of hierarchy in an organisation (*point made*). This means that messages have to pass between many intermediaries to go from the 'top' to 'bottom' of the organisation (*explanation*). Messages are more likely, therefore, to be distorted or be slow to arrive. This is why many firms have recently delayered (*analysis*).

The answer above provides a logical chain of thought: the number of levels of hierarchy affects the number of intermediaries involved in passing a message from 'top' to 'bottom' and this may affect the quality of the communication.

A second example is shown below.

Question: *Analyse the factors which might affect an individual's style of management.*

Answer: An individual's management style may depend on the nature of the employees (*point made*). If employees are untrained in a particular task they will need to be told what to do (*explanation*). An autocratic style might be more appropriate in this situation in order to get the task completed. Whereas if employees have a good understanding of the task and have specialist skills, the manager may adopt a more democratic style (*analysis*).

Again the thought process is logical: if employees do not know what to do, they may need to be told. If they themselves have specialist knowledge, the manager is more likely to ask for advice and information.

## What is synthesis?

Synthesis occurs when an answer is *structured effectively*. Essentially, it involves writing well organised answers rather than leaving it up to the reader to make sense of the argument. In a 'discussion' question this means putting an argument for a case, an argument against and then a conclusion.

Synthesis tends to come from planning your answer, rather than starting writing immediately. Whenever you face a question, try to sort out what you want each paragraph to say before you begin to write the answer out in full. This should lead to a better organised response. A final paragraph to bring together the arguments is also recommended.

## What is evaluation?

Evaluation is the highest skill and involves demonstrating some form of *judgement*. Once you have developed various points you have to show which one or ones are most important or under what circumstances these issues are most likely to be significant. Evaluation involves some reflection on the arguments for and against and some thought about which aspects are most important.

This often involves standing back from your argument to decide what would make your ideas more or less relevant. Ask yourself under what circumstances would one course of action be chosen rather than another. This process is illustrated below.

Question: *Discuss the possible gains from spending more on recruitment.*

Answer: Spending more on recruitment may mean the firm has a better selection of employees to choose from (*point made*). With more money being spent, it may be possible to search more widely and promote the vacancies more succesfully (*explanation*). This may mean that better candidates are selected which may improve the firm's performance. For example productivity may be higher, training costs may be lower and decision-making may be more informed (*analysis*). However, this does not depend purely on the amount spent. It also depends on how effectively the money is spent – for example, spending more on advertising the vacancy will not necessarily generate better applicants if the advertising is not targeted effectively. Also it will depend on external factors such as the state of the labour market; if there are few unemployed workers, then even if more money is spent it may still be very difficult to recruit (*evaluation of points*).

To evaluate your arguments you need to think carefully about whether the points you have made earlier in your answer are *always* true. What makes them more or less true? What makes the impact more or less severe? To what extent can the firm avoid or exploit the situation you have described? To evaluate effectively you have to imagine different organisations and think about what factors would influence them to act in one way or another. What would make the impact of change greater or smaller? Evaluation, therefore, requires a broad appreciation of the factors which influence a firm's decisions and an awareness of the variety of organisations present in the business world.

We hope you find these books useful. They are designed to be very different from typical textbooks in that they will help you use ideas and think about their importance. At the same time, these books will provide you with new ideas about topics and, we hope, will convey some of the passion and enthusiasm we have for such a fascinating subject.

CHAPTER 1

# Introduction and overview

## *Introduction*

For most modern businesses (small or large, manufacturing or service) the workforce is a major and important asset. A business's employees do not figure on the balance sheet, but few managers would underestimate the importance of people in creating and maintaining a thriving and competitive business. This book will consider the ways in which firms manage their employees and the factors that may influence all issues relating to the human dimension of business. One of the most fascinating aspects of studying people within organisations is the diversity of approaches, opinions and practices that can be encountered.

**If people are managed effectively they are likely to make a major, positive contribution to the organisation. Managed badly they are likely to resist change, have low productivity, produce poor quality work and deliver inadequate customer service.**

## *Key topics in people and organisations*

This book will consider the major theoretical aspects of people in organisations, as well as looking in detail at a number of issues relating to people and the organisations in which they work.

The key elements of people and organisations can be classified as follows:

- *Leadership and management style* – there is a spectrum of leadership styles that managers may adopt. **Authoritarian**, **democratic** and **laissez-faire** are frequently quoted leadership styles and we will also look at Douglas McGregor's **Theory X** and **Theory Y**. Although often presented as theories of motivation, McGregor was, in fact, writing about how a leader viewed his or her employees. Leadership style is a major influence on the way a business organises itself, the manner in which its employees communicate and the culture pervading the organisation.
- *Motivation of employees* – this is an important aspect of managing people and one in which there has been significant change over recent years. The approach of many Western businesses to managing and organising their staff has been strongly influenced by Japanese working practices – the so-called **Japanese approach**. The techniques employed by major businesses to motivate their staff have moved on from pay systems, job rotation and enrichment and more soph-

isticated approaches are now used. Many enlightened businesses organise their employees into teams and give the teams a high degree of control over their working lives. Such employees frequently organise their own methods of working, solve their own problems and propose changes to working practices.

**PROGRESS CHECK**

**Identify two factors that might indicate whether or not a workforce was highly motivated.**

**KEY TERM**

**A flexible workforce** is responsive to different market conditions. Such a workforce will contain multi-skilled employees able to switch between tasks, as well as part-time and temporary workers.

- *The structure and culture of the organisation* – the structure of an organisation is relatively straightforward to understand. Some organisations have many levels of hierarchy (or layers) and are formal and bureaucratic in their operation. Others have eliminated a number of layers of management and have sought to pass authority to those lower down the organisation. For some organisations a **matrix structure** is more appropriate – using multi-skilled project teams to carry out major tasks. The structure adopted by any organisation will, in some way, reflect the culture of the business. The culture of an organisation is the (perhaps unwritten) code that affects the attitudes, decision-making and management style of all its staff. Business cultures can be lively and youthful and perhaps goal-orientated, or they may be traditional and hierarchical. In any event, the culture of the organisation and its structure are likely to be interdependent.
- *Communications* – although most people accept the importance of good communication in business, communication problems still affect most organisations. Even with the tremendous developments in information and communications technology which have occurred in recent years, employees still complain that they do not know what is happening, why it is happening, what they are supposed to do or whether they are doing the right thing. The management of information, therefore, remains a crucial issue in business; indeed, with the rapid change in markets, access to and distribution of information has become a vital competitive weapon. Firms which fail to keep up with change and which do not keep employees informed and involved may well fall behind the competition.
- *Human resource management* – this is the modern term applied to the function previously known as personnel management. Human resource managers have responsibility for using and developing a business's workforce in the most productive way. Human resource management attempts to persuade all managers that developing their human resources (their staff) is a part of their job, not simply the responsibility of the personnel specialists. Human resource management does, of course, encompass the traditional work of the personnel department (for example, recruitment, selection, training and appraisal) but it also places greater emphasis on development through training and career planning. For many businesses, a major objective of human resource management is to improve business competitiveness through the creation of a **flexible workforce**.

PROGRESS CHECK

## Questions

1 In what ways might the effective management of people improve a firm's performance?
2 How might the way people are managed differ:
- in the army compared to a football team?
- in a hospital compared to a supermarket?

Explain your reasoning.

FACT FILE

One of the first major companies to introduce delayering was the American giant, General Electric. Under the leadership of Jack Welch, the company removed five of its nine layers of management during the first part of the 1980s. The company's view at that time was that many layers of management hid mediocre performances by many managers.

# *Key themes in people and organisations*

In the last few pages, we have outlined the major *topics* covered by the 'People and Organisations' module of most A Level syllabuses. Underpinning this part of the syllabus are also a number of *themes* relating to the way businesses organise themselves and the ways in which they manage their staff. Later chapters in this book will develop these aspects in full. Some of the major themes are set out in brief below.

## Delayering organisations

**Delayering** a business simply means reducing the numbers of levels of hierarchy within the business. Since the 1980s, this has become a common practice in businesses throughout the Western world. Delayering can entail a radical restructuring of the organisation, removing layers of (middle) management. For many businesses reducing the number of managers is a means of reducing expenditure on wages – often a major element of the business's costs.

In part, the process of delayering is designed to shorten lines of communication in the hope of improving the flow of information within the organisation. In the 1990s this process was increasingly combined with policies such as empowerment and team-working to give employees greater influence.

## Employee empowerment

Delayering has reduced the number of managers in the typical organisation. This process has provided motivational opportunities for the workforce, in particular the chance to empower employees.

Empowerment gives employees more control over their working lives and the opportunity to contribute to decision-making within the organisation. Empowerment offers employees a degree of self-regulation: the freedom to decide what to do and how to do it. The expectation is that this will make working life more interesting and result in improved performance and corporate competitiveness.

The precise nature of empowerment varies according to the culture of the organisation, but a number of common themes have emerged:

- the breaking up of rigid departmental structures and a move towards flexible, task-orientated teams
- changing the role of the supervisor into that of 'team coach' or facilitator, thereby reducing the hierarchical nature of the position
- allowing empowered teams to play a role in decision-making and problem-solving
- offering bonuses on a team, rather than an individual, basis.

KEY POINTS

A business is more likely to adopt Japanese approaches to managing people if:

- it is exposed to the full force of international competition (in these circumstances a firm would benchmark against the best international working practices to ensure it remained efficient in global terms)
- there are few differences in products making price competitiveness (and labour efficiency) crucial
- governments encourage businesses to implement the most up-to-date practices to maintain the competitive position of the economy as a whole
- competitors have successfully adopted such practices.

PROGRESS CHECK

**Discuss how empowerment might improve the performance of a business.**

## Japanisation

This is a term summarising the Japanese approach to management and the inclination of Western firms to follow this approach. Although the Japanese way varies from company to company (particularly as its use has become widespread), it comprises a number of common features. One of the key elements is the importance placed on having a highly educated and highly trained workforce. The importance of the workforce is reflected in the adoption of **single status** whereby contractual differences between grades of employee are eliminated. Single status grants all employees similar holiday entitlements and access to the same facilities at work; they may even wear the same clothing. The idea is to eliminate the 'them and us' syndrome.

As part of the Japanese way, employees are given a key role in improving production methods and quality with **kaizen** (continuous improvement) **groups** playing a central role in the strategy. Responsibility for managing the human resource of the organisation is also spread more widely amongst managers and not restricted to those who fulfil a traditional personnel role.

## Flexible firms

Over recent years many businesses have adopted organisational structures which have allowed them to become more flexible and responsive. Such businesses generally employ several different types of employee.

**Peripheral workers**

- employed on part-time, temporary or zero hours contracts

**Core workers:**
- Highly (multi?) skilled
- Permanent contracts
- Highly paid
- Essential to the organisation

- relatively few employment skills
- employees will be used flexibly as market conditions dictate
- vulnerable to redundancy and/or short hours in less prosperous times

**Figure 1.1** Core and peripheral workers

- **Core employees** who are managers, technicians and skilled workers possessing the essential knowledge critical for the successful operation of a business. Because they are essential, the organisation encourages loyalty with secure, full-time employment at high salary levels and with good conditions and fringe benefits.
- **Peripheral workers** are those on the edges of an organisation's labour force. They may be employed part-time, on temporary contracts or on **zero hours contracts.** Frequently they are semi-skilled or unskilled.
- Many businesses have **outsourced functions** such as the provision of information and communications technology in the expectation of reducing costs and improving service quality.
- **External workers** do not count as employees as they are mainly self-employed or employed by other organisations. Such workers are hired for short periods to provide specialist skills or as part of a contracting-out process whereby other firms provide services such as security or cleaning.

FACT FILE

**A zero hours contract** gives an employee a contract of employment, but no regular hours. The required hours of work might be advised at the start of the week.

The increasing desire for flexibility by firms has seen an increase in the number of employees who could be described as peripheral and in relatively insecure employment. Professor Charles Handy believes that firms will increasingly prefer the flexibility and cost-effectiveness of peripheral employees as they face fiercer global competition.

## Teleworking or homeworking

Over 3 million Britons now work from home. Some of these workers carry out relatively unskilled tasks and they do not require technical equipment or support from other employees. Homeworkers knit many high quality woollen products sold in the UK.

**Teleworking** means working at home, but in this case linked to the office by instant communications such as telephone, fax and computer modem. Some UK businesses have already moved a long way down the road towards teleworking.

**Teleworking statistics**

The numbers involved in teleworking remain small. According to the Labour Force Survey, there were 256,000 more-or-less full time teleworkers in 1998. Using a wider definition, this number increases to about 1.1 million (this includes plasterers, joiners and glaziers who work from a home base).

Nevertheless the trend is increasing according to Alan Denbigh of the Telework Association. 'We have seen a 13 per cent increase in the number of teleworkers between 1997 and 1998,' he says, 'which I'd say is quite a substantial growth. And I'd expect the 1999 figures to show a similar increase. Almost 5 per cent of the working population are teleworking.'

Source: © Andrew Bibby/*The Guardian* (11 July 1999)

**Figure 1.2** Homeworking and teleworking in the UK, 1998

PROGRESS CHECK

## Questions

1 In what ways might the adoption of a flexible workforce improve the competitiveness of a firm?
2 Assess the case for and against a business employing a significant proportion of its employees as teleworkers.

# *Changing patterns of employment*

As suggested in the section on themes above, the pattern of employment within the UK (and the European Union) has changed significantly during the 1990s. Examination of the relevant statistics highlights a number of key features. These are illustrated in figure 1.3 below.

| INCREASING INVOLVEMENT OF WOMEN | 1997 | | 2007 |
|---|---|---|---|
| Female share of total employment | 46.5% | Up To | 48.2% |
| Female share of employees in employment | 49.7% | Up To | 51.7% |
| MORE WORKING PART-TIME | | | |
| Part-time share of employees in employment | 29.1% | Up To | 31.2% |
| MORE SELF-EMPLOYED | | | |
| Self-employed share of total employment | 13.0% | Up To | 15.2% |

Note: All figures exclude government trainees and the armed forces

**Figure 1.3** Trends in employment, 1997–2007
*Source: Business Strategies Ltd, 1997, ONS*

## The move towards part-time employment

The UK, along with the remainder of the European Union, has seen little growth in full-time employment during the period covered by figure 1.3. At the same time, part-time employment has risen steadily irrespective of the state of the economy.

The trend towards part-time employment has been seen in most sectors of the UK's economy, but has been prominent in the service industries. This is partly because of the nature of the work, but also because of the extension of the working week and the increasing employment of females. All of these factors (as well as the opportunity, in many cases, to pay lower wages) have contributed to this important trend.

NUMERICAL INVESTIGATION

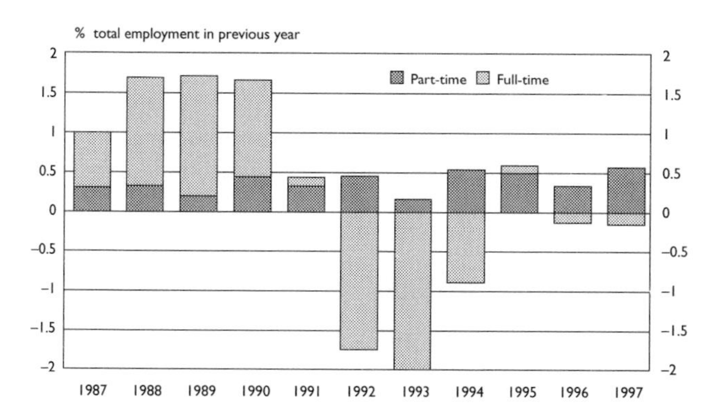


**Figure 1.4** Changes in part-time and full-time employment in the EU, 1987–1997. *Source: Employment in Europe, 1998/9 (European Commission)*

The data shows that full-time employment has fluctuated with the trade cycle, but that the relationship has weakened in the late 1990s. The loss of full-time jobs was particularly severe in 1993 when 2% of full-time jobs in the European Union were lost. In contrast, the growth in part-time employment has been maintained irrespective of the state of the economy.

a Consider the possible reasons why European businesses have chosen to employ part-time workers as the economy moved out of recession in the mid-1990s.
b Apart from their part-time status what other differences might employees recruited following the recession exhibit?

# The trend towards self-employment

Self-employed workers operate as their own bosses, either working **freelance** (working short-term for a variety of clients) or with the permanent task of running their own business. Self-employment offers tax advantages in comparison to regular employment and this is part of the attraction of this style of work.

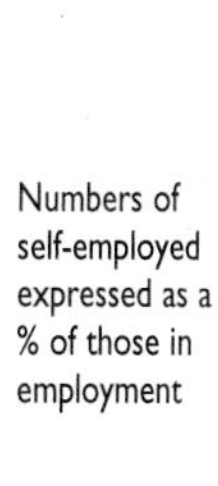

**Figure 1.5** Self-employment in the UK, 1975–1997
*Source: Employment in Europe 1998/9 (European Commission)*

Self-employment rose rapidly during the 1980s, peaking at 3.5 million people in 1990. Thereafter, the numbers of self-employed fell back, but are expected to rise again, exceeding 4 million by 2007.

The trend towards self-employment has been encouraged by the adoption of peripheral workers by businesses and the encouragement of an enterprise society by successive governments. Lack of opportunities for conventional employment has undoubtedly swelled the ranks of the self-employed.

The trend in the UK shown in figure 1.5 has been mirrored by developments throughout the European Union. In 1997, 15% of those in work across the Union were self-employed, compared with 12.6% for the UK.

## The increasing employment of females

Female employment accounted for virtually all of the rise in overall employment over the 15 years to 1999. The share of female employment rose from 41% of total employment in 1981 to 46.3% in 1998. Simultaneously, the number of males in full-time employment fell by 1.6 million. Women make up the majority of the labour force in financial and business services as well as the hotel and catering industries. These statistics reflect social changes in the UK as well as changes in employment creating job roles to which females are considered well suited.

NUMERICAL INVESTIGATION

The figures below relate to male and female employment (full-time, part-time or self-employed) in the UK over the period 1975 to 1997 (figures in millions).

| | 1975 | 1985 | 1990 | 1995 | 1997 |
|---|---|---|---|---|---|
| Males | 15.2 | 14.2 | 15.2 | 14.3 | 14.7 |
| Females | 9.4 | 10.1 | 11.6 | 11.6 | 11.9 |
| Total | 24.6 | 24.3 | 26.8 | 25.9 | 26.6 |

**Table 1.1** Changing employment. Source: *Employment in Europe, 1998/9 (European Commission)*

The trends here are clear. Over the 22 year period, the employment of females has risen steadily, whilst that of men has declined. At the same time the size of the workforce in the UK has risen.

Consider the changes in UK businesses which might have led to the trends shown in the table above.

## Other trends

There is a general trend towards temporary employment within the UK economy, again reflecting the desire of employers to improve competitiveness through the use of flexible workforces. At the same time there is a general trend towards businesses demanding increasingly skilled employees. This has been matched by increased use of highly sophisticated technology requiring greater skills on the part of workers.

**PROGRESS CHECK**

Examine ways in which recent changes in UK patterns of employment may affect a UK business.

# *Managing people*

Managing people is a critical aspect of a firm's success. Managed effectively, people can contribute significantly to the competitiveness of the organisation; managed ineffectively they can adversely affect its performance. Indicators such as **absenteeism**, **productivity** and **industrial action** all highlight the nature of employment relations within a firm. When people are managed well they embrace change, push the organisation forward and channel their energies, enthusiasm and commitment into their work. When they feel undervalued and are not motivated they can become a costly liability rather than an asset. The winners in business will be the firms which build and develop their employees' strengths. The losers will ignore their staff's abilities and waste their time and resources engaged in a relationship built on conflict rather than co-operation.

**NUMERICAL INVESTIGATION**

| MANAGERS REPORTING ABOVE AVERAGE: | INDUSTRIAL ACTION (AVERAGE NO. OF ACTIONS PER 100 WORKPLACES) | ABSENTEEISM (AVERAGE RATE PER 100 EMPLOYEES) | DISMISSALS (AVERAGE RATE PER 100 EMPLOYEES) | INDUSTRIAL TRIBUNALS (AVERAGE RATE PER 1000 EMPLOYEES) | FINANCIAL PERFORMANCE (% OF WORKPLACES) | LABOUR PRODUCTIVITY (% OF WORKPLACES) | QUALITY OF PRODUCT OR SERVICE (% OF WORKPLACES) |
|---|---|---|---|---|---|---|---|
| Manufacturing | 3.0 | 4.7 | 1.9 | 1.3 | 65 | 47 | 76 |
| wholesale and retail | 0.2 | 3.4 | 1.5 | 1.5 | 62 | 55 | 73 |
| transport and communications | 27.6 | 4.1 | 2.3 | 5.8 | 53 | 45 | 84 |
| financial services | 14.4 | 4.5 | 0.8 | 1.1 | 55 | 51 | 63 |
| public administration | 8.3 | 4.7 | 0.2 | 2.9 | 55 | 45 | 47 |
| health | 0.8 | 5.5 | 1.3 | 2.0 | 44 | 51 | 82 |
| **all workplaces** | **3.** | **4.1** | **1.5** | **1.7** | **57** | **50** | **74** |

*Source: Workplace–employee relations survey, Financial Times, 24 September 1999*

**Table 1.2** UK Workplace–employee relations survey 1999

a Which sector of the UK had the highest level of industrial action?
b Which sector of the UK had the lowest level of absenteeism?
c What costs might be associated with absenteeism?
d Which sector of the UK had the highest rates of dismissal? Why might this be?
e Which sector had the highest incidence of cases going to industrial tribunal? Why might this be?
f Does there seem to be any link between the managers' reports on employee performance and indicators such as absenteeism, industrial action, dismissals or tribunals?

# *Summary chart*

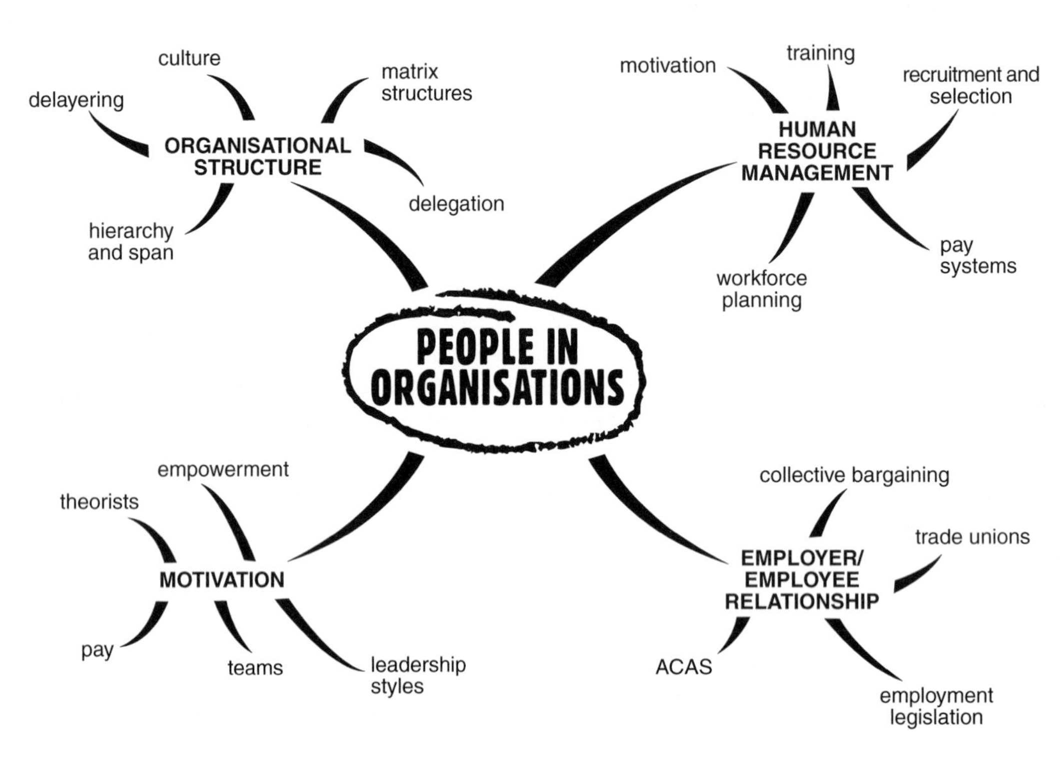


**Figure 1.6** Key elements of people and organisations

CHAPTER 2

# Leadership and management styles

## *Introduction*

One of the many interesting features of modern business is that the distinction between management and leadership is becoming increasingly blurred.

The conventional view of the role of managers is that they should *control* employees. By comparison, a leader has been seen as someone who gains the *trust* and *support* of other people; people follow the leader because they want to, not because they have to. A number of companies have attempted to bring these roles together and now present their managers as leaders. Rather than having control over employees, the new view of management tends to stress the importance of working *with* employees so that everyone shares the same goals. Major international businesses such as Levi-Strauss & Co have adopted this approach and place great emphasis on setting up and developing teams at all levels within the organisation. These teams operate through consensus, not authority. Throughout this chapter we will reflect the blurring of this distinction between 'leader' and 'manager' by using the terms interchangeably.

The move towards team-based management is a particularly important theme in business in the 21st century. We will return to it later in this chapter and again in Chapter 3 when we consider and assess team-working.

KEY TERMS

**Management**
is the process of setting objectives and making the most efficient use of financial, human and physical resources to achieve these objectives. Key tasks include planning, control and co-ordination.

**Leadership**
is influencing others to achieve certain aims or objectives. Effective leadership skills can help a manager to carry out their duties.

FACT FILE

Levi-Strauss, the US jeans manufacturer, has moved away from traditional management structures. The company relies heavily on teams rather than on direction from above. Information is made freely available to all employees. Teams hire employees and schedule their own work. One of the benefits of this change in management style has been the reduction of lead-time by 50%.

## *Leadership*

### What do leaders do?

Leaders or managers have a broad range of duties relating to all aspects of the business's operations. The tasks of leaders may include:

- *Deciding objectives for the organisation* – leaders have to establish a sense of direction for the organisation (often expressed in the mission statement). This is achieved by setting interim goals to move the organisation towards its overall aims.
- *Providing expertise and setting standards for the organisation* – the leader is required to show enthusiasm in difficult times and to take a major role in solving problems as they arise.

- *Drawing on all the expertise within the organisation* – the leader must utilise all team members' skills and experience when taking decisions.
- *Determining the structure of the organisation* – hierarchies and spans of control are at the leader's discretion. The leader will determine lines of communication and control, and will be instrumental in shaping the culture of the business.
- *Allocating rewards and punishment* – this is achieved through the design of pay and bonus systems, as well as the development of disciplinary procedures.
- *Acting as role models* – leaders set an example for other individuals within the organisation. They may choose to build alliances of senior individuals to protect their position.

Good leaders can push through change, provide vision, motivate and inspire. These qualities can have a significant impact on the success of a firm. Figures such as Richard Branson, Bill Gates, Jack Welch and Rupert Murdoch have all been described as great leaders in modern business; even though their styles differ considerably they all inject energy into their organisations, they lead the way and they inspire others. Good leaders energise their organisations enabling them to make great leaps in their development and to bring about significant change. They maintain momentum, enthusiasm and commitment.

# The changing nature of leadership

## Developments in ICT

Arguably, the nature of leadership has changed quite significantly over recent years. Rapid advances in information and communications technology have meant that managers have far more information available to them when making decisions. This can help them make better informed decisions, but it can also mean that managers have too much data and experience difficulty in identifying the key elements of a problem.

## Globalisation

The challenge faced by leaders has also been influenced by developments such as the creation of the Single European Market and increasing globalisation. This has meant, for many firms, that they operate in a larger and far more competitive environment. Decisions in such circumstances have become more complex. Some managers must attempt to organise production in a number of countries, facing a variety of languages, customs and cultures. Production difficulties are compounded by differing demands from customers across the world. The need to be innovative to ensure that the company's products and techniques do not become obsolete has added to the burden faced by leaders.

KEY TERM

**Culture**
is the attitudes, values and beliefs that normally exist within an organisation.

## Changes in organisational culture

The culture in which leaders operate has changed in many cases. Following instructions is simply not enough for many subordinates these days. In particular, many junior and middle managers are well trained and expect to be able to contribute to decision-making. The modern leader has to take into account their views and to broaden ownership of decision-making. Indeed, given the complexity of many modern organisations, the leader *relies* upon support from others in the management team. The increasing pace of change means that today's leaders have to be dynamic, flexible and able to respond effectively to changing environments. In particular, leaders of businesses providing technical products or services might experience and have to respond to rapid change.

**FACT FILE**

In Spring 1999, Stelios Haji-Ioannou, the founder and leader of EasyJet, decided to open warehouse-sized Internet cafés in London. These allow the public to eat and drink whilst surfing the net. Many commentators doubted the wisdom of this decision but the early success of the new cafés suggests that this reaction to a changing environment is, in fact, an appropriate one.

**PROGRESS CHECK**

**Do you think leadership is getting harder? Justify your answer.**

# *What makes a good leader?*

The general view of what constitutes a good leader has changed over time as the nature of the environment has evolved, new challenges have occurred, new tools and concepts have developed and individuals' attitudes have altered.

## The traditional view

The traditional view of a 'good' leader could be summarised as someone who:

- has a strong, decisive character
- is an 'expert' in the relevant field of business
- is an autocrat (to a significant degree)
- focuses on profits and financial success
- is a good communicator – but who is most comfortable with downward communication.

**FACT FILE**

'Most people in business assume that the chief executive is the supreme authority, a Caesar who freely directs, commands and controls,' says Sir Richard Evans. But when he took over at British Aerospace, he found 'that the power of the chief executive is often circumscribed, contingent and conditional'.
*Source: Financial Times, 18.08.99*

## The modern view

By comparison the modern view of a 'good' leader tends to stress someone who:

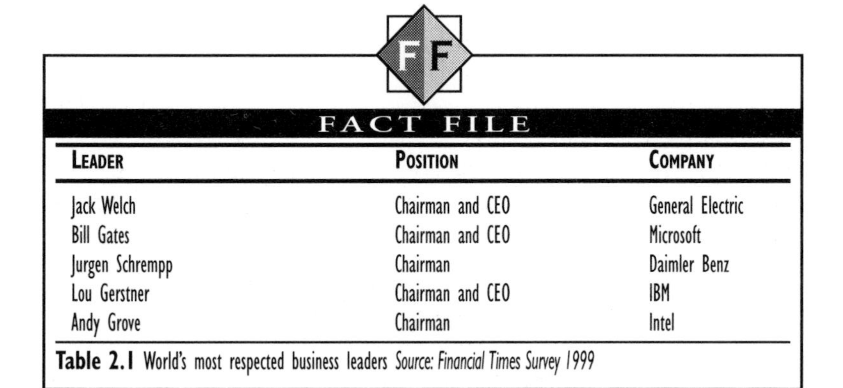

**FACT FILE**

| Leader | Position | Company |
|---|---|---|
| Jack Welch | Chairman and CEO | General Electric |
| Bill Gates | Chairman and CEO | Microsoft |
| Jurgen Schrempp | Chairman | Daimler Benz |
| Lou Gerstner | Chairman and CEO | IBM |
| Andy Grove | Chairman | Intel |

**Table 2.1** World's most respected business leaders *Source: Financial Times Survey 1999*

KEY POINTS

In the twenty-first century leaders and managers are more likely to:

- be democractic
- act as facilitators
- encourage two-way communication and discussion
- be able to respond quickly to change
- be flexible.

FACT FILE

In the late 1990s, Sir Brian Pitman helped to create the UK's biggest and most profitable high street bank. For many, he is the country's most successful banker in modern times. He first took control of Lloyds Bank in 1984 and turned one of the country's smallest clearing banks into one of the World's most profitable institutions. The deal which really made his name was the 1995 Lloyds merger with the TSB. Sir Brian Pitman is described as charming but fiercely competitive; a man who sets high standards for himself and all those who work for him.

FACT FILE

Several UK businesses faced a leadership crisis at the beginning of 1999. Cable & Wireless, Barclays Bank, EMI, Rank, United Utilities, National Grid, and BAA all had a vacancy at the highest level.

- is charismatic, with a flair for public relations
- possesses principles, for example trading ethically
- is an excellent communicator – this includes being a good listener
- welcomes advice and support from specialists
- is flexible and able to flourish in a changing environment

PROGRESS CHECK

**Discuss the characteristics of a 'good' leader.**

# *Theories of leadership*

Over the years, many theories have been presented concerning management and leadership and writers have put forward many ideas about what makes an effective leader. Views have changed over time and this has been reflected in the approaches to leadership adopted by businesses through history.

## Trait theories

Many writers have argued that all leaders should have a number of traits or characteristics, though there is some disagreement as to the precise nature of these traits. However, the consensus is that certain personality traits differentiate a good leader from other people. Trait theories have developed from the concept of the charismatic leader – Winston Churchill or John F. Kennedy would fall into this category. Examples like these have led to trait theory being termed 'great person theory'. Supporters of the idea of the charismatic leader contend that great leaders have identifiable characteristics that set them apart from ordinary people.

Some leadership traits commonly mentioned by writers include:

1. being informed and knowledgeable
2. having the ability to think creatively and innovatively
3. possessing inner motivation and the desire to achieve
4. having the ability to act quickly and decisively
5. projecting an air of authority
6. having first-class communication skills (including listening!).

### Are leaders born or made?

It is a matter of some debate as to whether it is possible to teach people the management skills associated with leadership or whether these traits are inherited by a lucky few. It is possible to argue that leaders do need to be born with some of the traits identified above, but also that some may be acquired through training. Equally, it is important to appreciate that the skills required to be a good leader vary according to the circumstances. Leaders require different skills to lead different groups of people and to work in different businesses. We consider this approach in more detail later in this chapter when we look at leadership style versatility.

PROGRESS CHECK

We have seen that many writers agree that managers or leaders need certain traits – or skills – to be successful. What is more controversial is the precise nature of the traits that leaders require.

## Questions

1 Which leadership traits may be important in the following circumstances:

- The manager of a large company is coping with widespread media allegations that their products are damaging to the health of consumers.
- The leader of a long-established, medium-sized, family business is suffering from successive years of poor trading?

2 To what extent does your answer to question 1 help you to narrow down which traits are *common* to all good leaders?

3 Assume the trait theorists are correct in their assertions. Discuss the implications this might have for an organisation's recruitment and selection process.

KEY POINTS

**Appropriate circumstances for autocratic style:**

- When a rapid decision is needed – perhaps in an emergency.
- When it is important that the same message is given out by everyone in the organisation – maybe as part of crisis management.
- When managers are responsible for a large number of (possibly unskilled) subordinates.

**Inappropriate circumstances for an autocratic style:**

- When taking highly complex decisions requiring diverse knowledge and skills.
- When leading a talented, self-motivated and creative group of employees.
- In circumstances in which junior managers are expected to develop a full range of managerial skills.

# *Style theories*

## A style continuum

The origins of the so-called style theories of leadership lie in the work of Lewis, Lippin and White who carried out extensive research in the 1940s. Their ideas have attracted much attention during the intervening years. Conventionally, leaders have been classified as being autocratic, democratic, paternalistic or laissez-faire (literally 'leave alone'). In reality it is not so simple. These four styles of leadership actually represent a continuum of styles and it is more accurate to think of a *spectrum* of leadership styles, from autocratic through to democratic.

One of the key factors in differentiating between leadership styles is communication. At the autocratic (or authoritarian) end of the spectrum communication is likely to be *downward*, as the leader or manager 'instructs' his or her subordinates to do their duties. Democratic leadership is more likely to result in *two-way communication*: consultation and 'selling' of the final goal are important. Laissez-faire leadership may result in relatively little communication: the problem or task may be outlined with subordinates who have considerable freedom thereafter.

### Autocratic or authoritarian leadership

Autocratic leadership is also sometimes termed authoritarian leadership. It refers to a leadership or management style which assumes that information and decision-making are best kept at the top of the organisation. It is also characterised by one-way communication (downward), minimal delegation or decentralisation and, frequently, close supervision of employees. Under this style the leader determines objectives, allocates tasks and expects obedience from subordi-

**FACT FILE**

Sir Clive Thompson, Chief Executive of Rentokil Initial, acknowledges that he runs his company along military lines, with eight layers of management between himself and a service operative (a shop-floor worker). Sir Clive expects communication to take place formally, with each level of hierarchy passing on the message to the next level.

**KEY POINTS**

An authoritarian leadership style is most likely when:

- the leader does not want to discuss issues
- a decision must be made quickly
- the decisions involve a high degree of risk
- the decisions involve a high degree of secrecy
- employees lack the necessary skills or desire to take decisions
- the group does not work well together
- the task is relatively straightforward needing little discussion.

nates. In these circumstances employees become very dependent upon their leaders as they do not have the necessary information (or confidence) to act on their own initiative.

Organisations managed in an authoritarian style frequently face various difficulties. Orders are passed down a chain and mistakes often result in criticism or disciplinary action. Hence, people avoid making decisions: matters to be decided are either passed up to a higher level, or decisions are made by committees (it is more difficult to dismiss all the members of a committee for jointly making a wrong decision). People survive by becoming expert at passing the buck. Senior management tends to be overworked, and staff turnover tends to be high.

Autocratic or authoritarian management can be an appropriate strategy under certain circumstances (see Key Points). However, in a modern, fast-moving organisation it is unlikely to benefit the firm.

As with all the conventional leadership classifications, the term 'autocratic manager' covers a range of actual styles. Extreme autocratic management will result in subordinates having no freedom of action. More benevolent autocratic leadership will allow for the possibility of some discussion or persuasion. This implies that limited two-way communication may occur.

As we have seen, autocratic leadership is not always the wrong approach. In some circumstances it may represent the best leadership style.

Surprisingly, there is evidence to suggest that some managers have become more autocratic in the 1990s. Companies such as Rentokil possess a business culture in which hierarchy is still regarded as important and communication is not always easy. Such organisational structures and cultures do not encourage the implementation of empowered teams.

**PROGRESS CHECK**

**Examine the possible reasons why managers might become more authoritarian in their approach.**

## Paternalistic leadership

A paternalistic leadership style is often practised in long-established businesses with low staff turnover. Paternalistic leadership is autocratic in approach but leaders take decisions in what they consider to be the best interests of the workforce. In these circumstances, leaders will explain decisions and may engage in limited delegation. However, paternalistic leaders are unlikely to delegate in such a way as to empower their workforces.

The paternal company treats its workforce as family, and places great emphasis on the social and leisure needs of its staff. This approach was common in Victorian times with famous examples such as Rowntree and Cadbury. Both companies exhibited a strong social conscience and, to protect the weaker members of the communities, they established a number of social services within model towns or communities.

## Democratic leadership

Democratic leadership (sometimes called participative leadership) entails operating a business according to decisions agreed by the majority. Decisions may be agreed formally through a voting system, but more usually as a result of informal discussions. The following are typical features of democratic leadership:

- The leader delegates a great deal and encourages decentralisation.
- The leader and subordinates discuss issues and employee participation is actively encouraged.
- The leader acts upon advice, and explains the reasons for decisions.
- Subordinates have greater control over their own working lives.

The successful operation of this style requires excellent communication skills on the part of the leader and the ability to generate effective two-way discourse. A considerable amount of management time may be spent on communicating in one form or another. This approach helps to develop the skills of subordinates and generally results in a more satisfied workforce.

Democratically-led groups usually have low dependency on their leader, offer constructive ideas and suggestions and derive great satisfaction from their employment. As a consequence, such groups have high levels of self-motivation and may require relatively little supervision.

There has undoubtedly been a move towards democratic leadership in many businesses over recent years (though some may argue that there are still many autocratically-led businesses around). This trend towards democratic leadership has a number of possible causes:

- *Society has changed* – business reflects society. People (that is employees) are less likely to be unquestioningly obedient.
- *Management theory* – this has developed and provided substantial evidence that people are more likely to be motivated (and productive) by the involvement resulting from the use of a democratic leadership style.
- *Leadership has become more complex* – businesses are larger and more complicated organisations; the environment in which they operate is dynamic and subject to rapid change. Individuals are more likely to need the support that democratic leadership provides in order to succeed in these circumstances.

There is a temptation to assume that democratic leadership is the 'best' style. This is rather simplistic, as with any other style it is appropriate in some circumstances.

**KEY TERMS**

**Delegation**
means passing authority down the hierarchy. This is only genuine if the manager relinquishes some control to the subordinate.

**Empowerment**
provides subordinates with the means to exercise power over their working lives. Whilst empowerment gives subordinates a large degree of control over their working lives, delegation tends to relate to a *specific task* or activity.

**FACT FILE**

One of Britain's best-known companies was run for many years along paternalistic lines. The company originally milled flour and was managed by three generations of the Rank family. Even after the business expanded in the 1950s, taking over the Hovis bakery business and becoming Rank Hovis, the Chairman, Joseph Rank, still led the company in a paternalistic style.

**PROGRESS CHECK**

**Consider the possible impact on employees of a change from an authoritarian to a democratic style of leadership.**

KEY POINTS

**Democratic leadership is most appropriate when:**

- the workforce is highly skilled
- complex decisions and activities are undertaken
- leaders are willing to delegate authority extensively to subordinates.

**Democratic leadership is less appropriate when:**

- quick decisions are required
- the workforce is relatively unskilled
- a traditional, hierarchical structure exists within the organisation.

KEY POINTS

The laissez faire management style may most likely be adopted when:

- the managers do not care
- the managers do not think they have any effect on employees' performance
- managers want to liberate the workforce
- the workforce is perfectly capable of completing the task unaided.

## Laissez faire leadership

This approach is sometimes described as mild anarchy! Under this approach the leader has a minimal input into the operation of the business. Staff take the majority of the decisions with little reference to the leader. As a consequence, the organisation can lack a sense of direction and exhibit poor co-ordination and planning.

The laissez faire style of leadership may occur because of the shortcomings of the leader; they may lack the essential skills needed to carry out the role successfully. Alternatively, it may be a conscious and brave policy decision to give staff the maximum scope for using their capabilities. It can be an appropriate style to adopt in certain circumstances. For example, the leader of a highly creative team may deliberately adopt this style in the expectation of bringing out the best in his or her subordinates.

Laissez faire leadership may be successful in the following circumstances:

- The manager or leader is one amongst a number of equals in terms of experience and qualifications.
- The workforce is self-motivated and understands the position adopted by their managers.
- The workforce understands and agrees with the organisation's objectives.

Laissez faire leadership tends to result in highly independent employees who are willing to voice their opinions. Staff may be satisfied or dissatisfied with this style of leadership, depending on their skills, the complexity of the tasks to be completed and the personality of the leader.

PROGRESS CHECK

**A firm is in financial difficulty and is considering redundancies. Discuss how the leadership style of the firm's managers may affect the external decision and the process by which it is made.**

## Style versatility

Building on the idea that there is not a single perfect style of leadership, it is possible to argue that the best managers are those who adopt a style suitable to the circumstances. Thus, the most talented managers are the most versatile, able to call on one or more of the styles we have discussed, having assessed the demands of the situation.

Therefore, a versatile manager might adopt a democratic approach when reaching a decision on a proposed marketing campaign with a small group of writers and artists. A more paternalistic style may be adopted when dealing with a larger, long-serving group of shop-floor employees.

Two American scholars, Victor Vroom and Paul Yetton, developed this approach further. Their model of leadership is based on the idea that leaders are adaptable and versatile. This model proposes that effective leaders should act according to the situation in which they find themselves. In particular, the model concentrates on the degree of involvement in decision-making that subordinates can have and relates this to the circumstances surrounding the decision.

Assuming that the 'best' managers adopt a versatile style of leadership, this has a number of implications:

1 There is a greater need for management training to assist leaders in recognising the need for different styles of management in different situations (more autocratic when dealing with inexperienced and untrained colleagues for example). Leaders also need help to develop the skills used in different management styles.
2 A more flexible and task-orientated culture may be needed within businesses to respond to the varying management styles. A paternalistic organisation might experience problems, for example, if authority is suddenly devolved to a shop-floor team.
3 Subordinates might find it difficult to work with a manager who seems to change styles according to the circumstances. They may require training to enable them to fulfil roles requiring greater autonomy.

**FACT FILE**

Research at Chiltern University has shown that subordinates consider humour to be more important than intelligence in a leader. The findings suggested that humour can help to improve morale and productivity in the workplace.

**PROGRESS CHECK**

## Questions

1 Consider the skills that a versatile manager might need to operate successfully.
2 Do you think most managers are likely to be able to adjust their style of management according to the situation facing them?

## Factors influencing choice of leadership style

A number of factors might influence the leadership style chosen by a manager.

- *The personality of the leader* – a confident, good communicator would be well suited to a democratic style of leadership, whereas a decisive individual who prefers to be in control is more likely to be autocratic in approach.
- *The type of labour force* – highly trained and confident employees will have more to offer and will respond better to democratic leadership. The same will not be true of large groups of relatively unskilled employees.
- *The nature of the task and the timescale* – if the task is urgent then autocratic leadership might be appropriate; if it requires a highly creative input, it might be managed best by a laissez faire approach.
- *The culture and tradition of the business* – organisations develop their own pattern of behaviour over time. An organisation with a tradition of paternalistic leadership would put pressure on new managers to conform to this way of thinking.

**PROGRESS CHECK**

## Questions

1 Analyse the factors which might determine the right style of leadership at any particular moment.
2 To what extent does the personality of a manager determine his or her style of management?

# *Douglas McGregor's Theory X and Y*

KEY POINTS

A Theory Y manager is likely to believe that:

- workers seek satisfaction from employment, not just a pay cheque
- workers possess knowledge, creativity and imagination
- workers willingly commit themselves to organisational objectives
- poor performance by employees is due to repetitive and monotonous work or poor management
- employees wish to contribute to decision-making.

Douglas McGregor was an American social psychologist who researched into management in large companies. His writing developed understanding of leadership by considering how the attitude of the leader might shape his or her behaviour towards employees. He published *The Human Side of Enterprise* in 1964. McGregor's book has received much acclaim and particular attention has centred on his comparison of two types of leader as set out in Theory X and Theory Y.

His research revealed that many leaders assumed their workers were motivated solely by money and had no innate desire to work. McGregor referred to this type of manager as a **Theory X** leader. He also discovered an alternative and less common type of manager, which he termed a **Theory Y** leader. Such leaders, according to McGregor, believed workers sought more than financial gain from employment. Thus, a poor performance by a group of workers may be the result of a work environment lacking stimulation and challenge for employees. The behaviour of employees, argued McGregor, is often the result of the way they are treated.

**Theory X and Theory Y refer to how managers view their employees – they do not necessarily describe the employees.**

KEY TERM

**Piece-rate pay**
operates when employees are paid according to the quantity they produce. Thus, a fruit-picker might receive a certain payment for every box of fruit picked.

McGregor did not believe in the views expressed by Theory X leaders. He proposed Theory X so that he could disprove it as part of his support for the views expressed by Theory Y managers.

Theory X is derived from the work of F. W. Taylor and the Scientific School of management who contended that workers were 'economic animals' motivated solely by money. Theory X leaders seek to get the best from their employees by use of techniques such as piece-rate pay and close supervision. It is likely that a Theory X approach could be self-fulfilling. If a manager does not trust his or her employees and, as a result, fails to delegate they may well lose interest in the work. This will convince the manager that he or she was right not to give the subordinates any additional authority!

Theory Y, by comparison, stems clearly from Mayo's human relations approach and Maslow's work on human needs (these theories deal with motivation and are discussed in Chapter 3). Theory Y focuses on meeting the social and psychological needs of individuals within the workplace. McGregor's work is, however, a theory of leadership and *not* one of motivation.

If leaders adopt a Theory Y style the implications can be significant for a business:

- Greater delegation within the organisation allows those further down the hierarchy to have greater authority.
- Training for managers encourages delegation and improves two-way communication.
- Reviewing the business's culture discourages managers from retaining what they might see as their 'authority'.

- Considering the organisation's structure and considering approaches such as delayering can be positive.

A business moving towards a Theory Y approach to leadership requires planning, the support of its managers and shop-floor workers and considerable training for all the employees involved.

FACT FILE

British leaders are changing their approach to management according to recent research by academics at Nene University. They no longer rely on the 'old boy network' but are adopting modern techniques such as delegation. The researchers also gave British managers a pat on the back – apparently they are less bureaucratic and consult their employees more than their American equivalents.

PROGRESS CHECK

## Questions

1 **Discuss the possible benefits of the Theory Y approach for a firm.**
2 **'A Theory X approach is self-fulfilling.' Discuss.**
3 **Examine the factors which might cause a manager to adopt a Theory Y approach.**

# *Team-based management*

Team-working occurs when production is organised into large units of work, instead of requiring workers to each complete a specialised task repetitively. The team of people is likely to be working on a large task such as installing all electrical components into a car. For teams of workers to carry out complex tasks successfully it is essential that they are:

1 given a high degree of empowerment to carry out their duties
2 well trained and also multi-skilled
3 allowed time to discuss problems and solutions as well as to set their own targets
4 motivated by something more than the piece-rate rewards.

FACT FILE

**Quality circles** are small groups of employees, drawn from all levels of the organisation, who meet regularly to identify problems and discuss solutions.

**Kaizen groups** are similar to quality circles but comprise mainly shop-floor employees.

This style of management is in stark contrast to traditional styles in which managers simply instruct workers in their duties. It places great emphasis on delegation of authority to shop-floor employees and may entail the removal of some layers of management to allow employees more control over their working lives. Team-working has its roots in Japanese working practices and, in particular, techniques such as **quality circles**.

Team-based leadership may also require the implementation of single status into the workplace. As discussed earlier, single status entails the removal of all barriers distinguishing between different grades of staff within the organisation. Thus, all employees use the same canteen and other facilities, work similar hours, have similar holiday arrangements and wear the same clothing. The only remaining distinction should be the level of pay received by the various grades in the organisation.

## Managing successful teams

Writers, including Charles Handy, have argued that managing teams successfully involves a number of key factors. Part of the art of leading a team to achieve success is to ensure that the *balance* of the team is correct. To attain corporate objectives, a team must have individuals who can, between them, carry out a range of duties. Team members must be multi-skilled and their personalities must be *complementary* rather than merely similar. Thus, successful teams need people with drive and motivation, but also people with administrative skills to ensure that all relevant tasks are completed properly. So, an important part of managing a team is to ensure that the right blend of individuals is incorporated into the group.

FACT FILE

Alan Sugar, Chairman of the household electronics group Amstrad plc, announced that his group returned to profitability in 1998 for the first time in 4 years. The key to the improvement appeared to have been the re-establishment of the engineering team that produced a range of successful products in the 1980s.

KEY POINTS

Team-based management is more likely to succeed if:

- the team has the right mix of people
- the culture of the organisation is team-based
- organisational objectives are clear
- employees are well trained.

## Co-ordinating teams within an organisation

Teams can become complacent, confident in their own success and unaware of major changes taking place outside the team. This can result in failure to achieve targets. Successful team-based management may, therefore, require regular changes in the personnel of teams to ensure that external factors receive sufficient attention and that the focus of the team does not switch inwards.

It is important for leaders to make sure that all the teams within an organisation are pulling in the same direction in pursuit of the organisational objectives. Teams may target goals that are different from the corporate objectives or may become too competitive. The desire to beat a rival team may become more important than meeting key performance indicators. Senior managers have to ensure that the competitiveness inherent between, as well as within, teams is channelled solely into achieving the organisation's objectives.

Businesses contemplating the introduction of team-based management need to consider:

- the training implications both at managerial and shop-floor level
- the extent to which the culture of the organisation may need to change
- the fact that managers will not automatically relinquish control
- that teams need to be carefully constructed
- the short-term disruption to production which is likely.

We consider team-working in more detail in Chapter 3.

PROGRESS CHECK

**Discuss the possible benefits of a team-based management approach.**

# *Does leadership matter?*

This is an important question. Does it really matter to a business whether they have highly skilled and conscientious leaders? As in so many cases, the answer to this question will depend upon the circumstances.

Good leadership is really important:

- in a highly competitive market where profit margins are slim
- in the early stages of a business's life when it is attempting to establish itself
- at a time of particularly rapid and substantial change
- at a time of crisis – for example if consumers lose confidence in a product, or a take-over is threatened.

Good leadership may be desirable, but is not so critical:

- when a business is well established with strong brands and high levels of consumer loyalty

- in a market where patterns of demand change infrequently
- when the workforce are highly skilled and motivated – the role of the leader might be more administrative in these circumstances.

Obviously, there are times when effective leadership may be absolutely crucial (such as in times of crisis) but it is also true to say that good leadership is *always* important for the long-term success of any organisation. Even a business with a strong market share, high profits and well-established brands may find its position declining unless appropriate decisions and actions are taken. Rivals may develop new, more sophisticated products which are highly valued by consumers. Sales and profits may diminish and the firm's position in the market declines. A business (or a leader for that matter) should not take success for granted. Effective leadership provides direction and ensures organisations remain competitive now and in the future.

It may be argued that leaders should be developed throughout the organisation. A business led by one strong individual may flounder when that person moves on. This is a common problem for firms which have been built up by the founder, perhaps someone with a strong hands-on approach, who then retires. For long-term success, leadership skills need to be deeply rooted in and valued by the organisation. An advantage of team-based managment is that the firm does not become too reliant on any single individual.

## A successful leader

How can we judge if an individual is successful in their role as a leader? A number of factors may be taken into consideration when making such an assessment.

Perhaps the most obvious measurement of leadership performance is the extent to which the organisation meets its objectives. Thus, the chief executive of a large financial services organisation might be deemed to be succeeding if the company increases the value of the business or expands its market share – if these were the stated objectives for the organisation. Modern leaders often receive financial rewards (sometimes in the form of share options) for achieving such targets.

An alternative measure might be to analyse the workforce. It is plausible to argue that a successful leader would generate high levels of motivation amongst staff. As a result of this it would be reasonable to expect low levels of labour turnover, little industrial action and declining rates of absenteeism.

Some would argue that the degree of success of leadership can be measured in financial terms. Not only would rising profits be expected, but also tight control of costs, increasing revenues and perhaps an improving return on capital.

Other measures of success might include being able to attract other, talented and highly regarded employees due to the reputation of the business and its leader. Equally, if the leader is the target of headhunters from other firms it may be deduced that he or she has done a good job.

PROGRESS CHECK

## Questions

1 Why might leadership be particularly important for a small firm planning to develop and sell computer software for businesses?
2 Consider how the success of an autocratic manager might be judged over a period of time.

# *Summary chart*

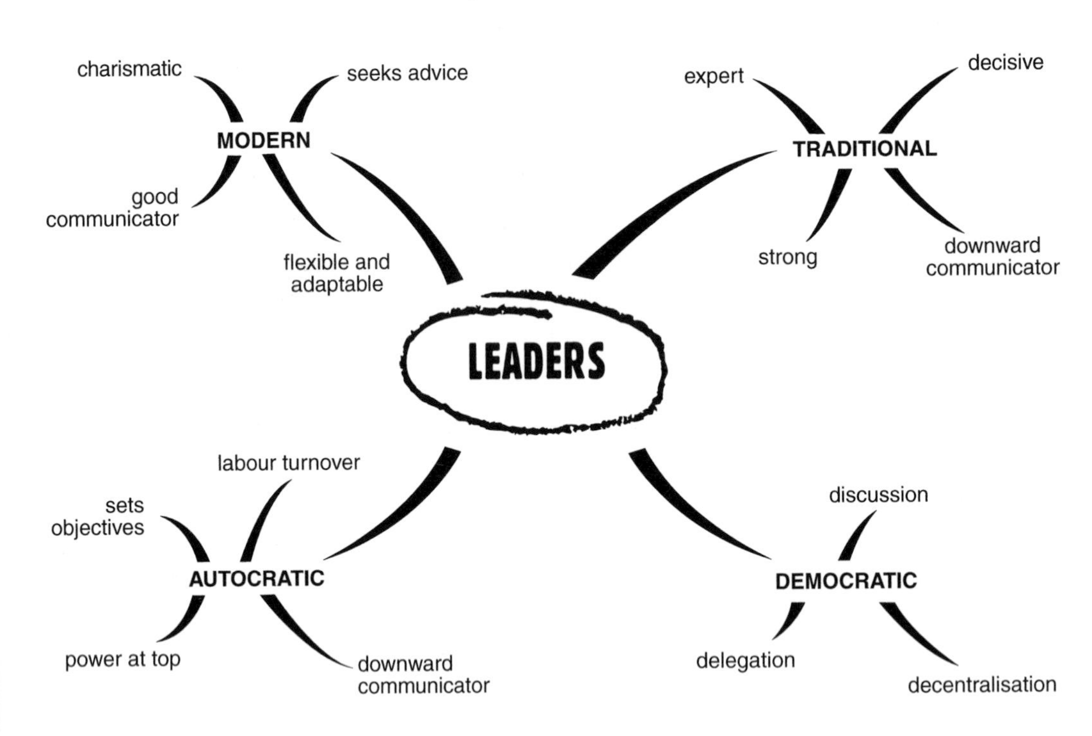


Figure 2.1 Key elements in leadership and management styles

# Approaching exam questions: Leadership

## 'Advances in Information Technology have made the task of the leader more difficult in today's business world.' To what extent do you agree with this statement?

**(40 marks)**

The use of the phrase 'To what extent ...' in this question emphasises that you must look at both sides of the argument. So, you could say that there are several reasons why advances in Information Technology (IT) have made a leader's role more testing:

- More information is available on which to base decisions, which sometimes results in overload.
- Some leaders do not have sophisticated IT skills and do not feel in control of the situation. They have to rely on others to help them with this aspect.
- Changes in IT have hastened the pace of change (assisting in implementing systems such as JIT for example) and this makes the role of the leader more challenging.

There are also arguments against this view. IT allows leaders to communicate quickly and effectively with colleagues and this is critical for businesses which increasingly operate in a global environment. IT has offered new trading opportunities (for example the Internet) which some managers have been quick to grasp.

It really depends on whether leaders view IT as a threat or an opportunity, the level of IT training available to support leaders and the style of leadership used.

## Andrew Parkinson has been Chief Executive and Managing Director of Hales Engineering for 5 years. During that time the company has experienced declining sales and the workforce has been reduced by 30%, yet Mr Parkinson has enjoyed a 150% increase in pay. Some stakeholders have called for his resignation. Discuss whether or not the critical stakeholders may have a case.

**(40 marks)**

There is more to this statement than meets the eye initially. A number of key questions have to be addressed:

- What were the business's objectives during this time – perhaps they were rationalisation and cost reduction?
- What was the initial level of pay granted to the Chief Executive and what has happened to pay for senior managers generally over this period?

- Who are the stakeholders who have voiced criticisms? For shop-floor employees to hold such views is not unusual whilst shareholders expressing them could be a worry.
- What has happened to the market for this firm's products over the 5 years? If it has been declining generally this performance might not be so damning.

This style of question offers you a little information and invites you to assess its worth. It is always worth putting the information you are given in context and considering *what else you need to know to make a reasonable judgement.* By adopting such an approach your answer will be evaluative.

## 'Circumstances are more important factors than personal attributes in the management of modern businesses.' Critically assess this statement.

**(40 marks)**

Examiners enjoy setting questions like this! They make a controversial statement and then invite you to assess its accuracy. The important point to appreciate is that the answer is always the same: the statement is true *to some extent.*

You should be able to able to offer arguments whereby *circumstances dictate* the management style to be used (an emergency requiring rapid decisions and an autocratic approach). This aspect of your answer will support the sentiments expressed in the quotation.

However, it is critical that you also address the other side of this issue. Leaders should develop personal strengths as part of their work. Thus, good communication skills and decisiveness might be important attributes irrespective of the circumstances.

The important final part of any answer to this question is to arrive at some sort of judgement. In what circumstances might personal attributes be particularly important? When could circumstances shape leadership style?

## 'Good leadership is essential if a business is to improve its performance.' To what extent do you agree with this statement?

**(40 marks)**

This is another wide-ranging essay question which addresses a number of important aspects.

It is possible to offer arguments on both sides of this essay and a good quality answer should attempt to do so. The benefits of good leadership could be explained in terms of improving productivity and profitability, or in terms of product range and industrial relations.

Equally, you could argue that many other factors affect the performance of a business – exchange rates, government policies and the actions of competitors are just a few.

An evaluative conclusion may centre on a number of issues.

- What is 'good' leadership?
- Is it a particular style, or is it a flexible approach?
- How do we measure the performance of a business?
- Are profits the best measure of successful leadership?
- Should we consider market style or labour turnover?
- What is the time scale over which we should make a judgement (for example, the statement in this question is likely to be true in the long-term)?

## Consider the view that modern managers should automatically adopt a democratic style of leadership.

**(11 marks)**

This is an apparently one-sided question, but it actually requires you to look behind the question and to say that democratic leadership is not always appropriate – it depends, as always, on circumstances.

You should offer one or two arguments in support of this case perhaps by examining situations in which:

- complex decisions are needed
- sufficient time is available to complete the task
- expert advice may be required
- the organisation has a culture of delegation and/or empowerment.

However, you should argue that there are many circumstances where other styles of leadership may be appropriate – with unskilled workers, when time is scarce and so on. One point that you may consider is that the term 'democratic leadership' covers a range of styles – it is not a single approach.

# Student answers: Leadership

## Evaluate the case for the manager of a scientific research department employing a laissez-faire style of leadership.

**(11 marks)**

### Student answer

A manager of a scientific research department might adopt a laissez-faire style of leadership for a number of reasons. He might not have the skills necessary for carrying out the role of a leader and may not have received any training. As a result he might automatically use the laissez-faire style as it involves him in fewer decisions.

He might also use this approach because his workforce is skilled and do not require a lot of instructions from him. This, then, might be the reason why he has chosen to just set out the task of the objective of their work and leave them to get on with it.

### *Marker's comments*

*This response is fairly typical of many students' answers. The student obviously understands the nature and shortcomings of laissez-faire leadership and also has some understanding of the circumstances in which it might be appropriate. However, the answer does not demonstrate a well-developed examination technique or a full understanding of what the question requires. One mistake was to rewrite the question as the first line of the answer. This is a common and time-wasting feature of many student answers.*

*Also, the answer is one-sided in spite of the clues given by the command word (evaluate) and the mark allocation (see mark scheme below). This question required an analysis of the case for and against the use of this style before attempting to make some judgement as to its validity.*

**Mark: Content 2/2, Application & Analysis 4/6, Evaluation 0/3. Total = 6**

## Discuss the ways in which the nature of the group being led might determine the leadership style employed.

**(11 marks)**

### Student answer

It is important that leaders take into account the nature of the people they are managing when deciding what type of leadership style to adopt. If leaders do not do this they may upset the group if, for example, they are used to being given a fair degree of control over their own affairs, and suddenly this is taken away.

Groups may also become annoyed if leaders change their approach because of circumstances, leaving them unsure of what they have to do.

It could also cause problems if leaders ignore the skills and qualifications of the workforce when choosing their management style. A leader might be very democratic and consultative with employees who lack skills and experience.

So, to summarise it is important that leaders take into account the nature of the people that they are leading when selecting a leadership style.

### Marker's comments

*This is a fairly typical response from a candidate who has some subject knowledge, but a limited examination technique. The student has little chance of achieving a high mark because the answer contains little or no analysis. The large number of brief paragraphs comprising this answer highlights this aspect of the response. The student did not develop the points, although he or she undoubtedly had some subject knowledge.*

**Mark: Content 2/2, Application & Analysis 2/6, Evaluation 0/3. Total = 4**

# Analyse the reasons why the managing director of a small factory might take a Theory X view of his workforce.

**(9 marks)**

## Student answer

A manager might take a Theory X view of his workforce because he knows little about them and has not spent time talking to them. He may not have been involved in their recruitment. He might not have been trained in management and may not treat people as individuals. Other managers in the factory might influence him in his opinions or they might always have viewed their workforce in this way. In any event it will not be beneficial to the business. He needs to change his ways.

### Marker's comment

*This is a very weak answer which displays a lack of subject knowledge as well as poor examination technique. It is unclear from this answer whether the student understands the meaning of '... a Theory X view of his workforce'. It would have been wise to commence with a statement showing an understanding of McGregor's Theory X.*

*From here, the candidate should have developed two or three arguments fully using separate paragraphs. The student made some good, general points – for example, a lack of management training could have been a valid line of argument.*

**Mark: Content 2/2, Application 0/4, Analysis 0/3. Total = 2**

# Consider whether the 'best' management style is a flexible one that varies according to the circumstances.

**(11 marks)**

## Student answer

There are several arguments to support the view that managers should vary their leadership style to suit the situation. Thus, a manager leading a highly complex and long-term project supported by highly trained and motivated subordinates might elect to use a democratic approach. This would be supported by two-way communication and would allow the manager to make effective use of the subordinates' skills and knowledge.

The leader of a large and relatively unskilled group may take a different view. He may consider that his employees need close direction and supervision to ensure that they continue to assist the business in reaching its objectives.

However, there are drawbacks to the style of leadership in which managers use varying approaches. It can be confusing for employees if they are unsure as to what the leader expects of them. On some occasions they will be told what to do, whilst at other times they will be consulted. This may, in fact, damage communication within the business.

### *Marker's comment*

*This is a good quality response. The student has developed the arguments well and has made effective use of paragraphs. Reading this answer it is apparent that the student has revised thoroughly and understands what the question requires.*

*A slight weakness is that the answer is a little unbalanced. The student appreciates the need to offer arguments on both sides of the case but has not provided a great deal of analysis on why this 'variable' style may not be the best available to managers.*

**Mark: Content 2/2, Application & Analysis 5/6, Evaluation 2/3. Total = 9**

# *End of section questions*

1 Analyse the likely sources of power for the owner–manager of a small retail business.
(9 marks)

2 To what extent might a manager's communication skills determine the style of leadership he or she adopts?
(11 marks)

3 Examine the ways in which we might judge whether the Chief Executive of a charity has performed successfully.
(9 marks)

4 Discuss whether an authoritarian style of management is likely to lead to the best results.
(11 marks)

5 Analyse the factors which might cause a manager to change his or her management style.
(9 marks)

6 Analyse the reasons which may have caused a small manufacturer to abandon its team-based approach to management.
(9 marks)

7 Consider the view that McGregor's Theory X and Theory Y is of little value as it only considers extremes.
(11 marks)

8 Discuss whether a leader can be both task-orientated and people-centred.
(11 marks)

9 Consider the view that the success of a leader can only be measured in the long-term.
(11 marks)

10 Discuss the view that a manager cannot succeed in a senior post without good leadership skills.
(11 marks)

# *Essays*

1 'Leaders are born, not developed.' Critically analyse this view.
(40 marks)

2 The managing director of Hendersons plc is at odds with the rest of his board of directors. He wishes to introduce empowered teams onto the shop floor. His co-directors believe that team-working is a fashion which does not offer long-term benefits. Consider the merits of the two arguments.
(40 marks)

3 The skills needed to manage a business are unchanging. A successful manager in the nineteenth century would flourish today. To what extent do you agree with this view?
(40 marks)

4 Many businesses today operate throughout the World and employ hundreds of thousands of people. In view of the scale of such organisations, individual leaders have relatively little impact upon the operation of a business. To what extent do you agree with this view?
(40 marks)

5 'High and increasing profits are a clear indication of the existence of a successful leader.' Discuss this statement.
(40 marks)

# Motivation, team-working and empowerment

## *Motivation of employees*

### What is motivation?

Motivation, in the context of employment, can be defined as the will to work due to enjoyment of the task itself. This implies that motivation comes from *within* the individual. Some writers regard motivation as the will or desire to achieve a given target or goal. This suggests that motivation has an important external dimension. This is a critical distinction.

KEY TERMS

A **time and motion study** or **work study** analyses the way in which jobs are carried out, including measuring the time taken for various duties. The aim is to make the most efficient use of human resources.

FACT FILE

Employers and employees still do not agree about what motivates people at work. A recent survey revealed that nearly 90% of employers believe that money is the main motivator whilst employees only rank pay fourth (behind interest, security and achievement).

### Motivational theories

| SCHOOL OF THOUGHT | KEY WRITERS | ESSENTIAL IDEAS |
|---|---|---|
| Scientific School | Frederick Winslow TAYLOR (1856–1917) | Believes motivation is an **external factor** achieved through money. Employees should be closely supervised and paid piece-rate. **Time and motion studies** were used to determine efficient means of production and workers had no input. |
| Human Relations School | Elton MAYO (1880–1949) | This brought sociological theory into management and proposed that employees could be motivated by addressing their **social needs**. More attention was given to the social dimension of work (e.g. communication, working in groups and using consultation between managers and employees). |
| The neo-Human Relations School of Management | Abraham MASLOW (1908–1970), Douglas McGREGOR (1906–1964), Frederick HERZBERG (1923–) | This school highlighted the importance of fulfilling **psychological needs** to improve employee performance. Motivation depended upon designing jobs to fulfil psychological needs. |

**Table 3.1** Schools of thought on motivation

Over the years, various schools of thought have developed. They differ fundamentally on *why* people work. Is it to gain money, to interact with other humans or to fulfil individual needs such as achievement and recognition? If managers can identify why people work they can determine how best to motivate them at work.

The techniques of motivation used by particular firms will reflect the beliefs of the managers and the culture of the individual organisations. Proponents of the Scientific School of Management, for example, would argue that external factors (particularly money) motivate employees. Others recognise that working practices, social groupings and individual needs are vital.

**KEY TERMS**

**Delegation**
is the passing down of authority (*but not responsibility*) through the levels of hierarchy of an organisation.

**Job rotation**
is a system whereby employees carry out a wider variety of tasks of similar complexity. They switch regularly from one task to another to reduce monotony.

**PROGRESS CHECK**

Employees have needs that cannot be met by monetary rewards. Obviously each person is different, but a number of common needs can be identified:

- recognition
- responsibility
- achievement
- personal growth.

With reference to the above list, analyse the ways in which a large manufacturing firm might motivate:
(a) its shop-floor employees and (b) its managers.

**PROGRESS CHECK**

How do the Scientific School and the Human Relations School differ in their view of employee motivation?

**Motivated employees are likely to be more committed, to put more energy into their work and to be more open to change. They want to achieve something at work.**

**FACT FILE**

Companies are increasingly making use of non-cash rewards to motivate individuals. These range from recognition in the form of a certificate, plaque or special awards dinner to being given additional responsibilities. The wide variety of rewards available means that the company can select the one that is appropriate to each individual.

## How can firms motivate employees?

Managers today can choose a variety of techniques to motivate their employees, from financial methods (bonuses and piece-rate pay, for example) to non-financial techniques such as job rotation or delegation. It can be relatively easy to motivate employees in the short-term; long-term motivation can be more difficult.

### Techniques for short-term and long-term motivation

*Short-term techniques*:

- praise
- a bonus (further bonuses motivate for even shorter periods of time)
- a social event for staff.

Most motivational techniques have some positive effects in the short-term. However, many managers may not realise that many techniques have a limited impact in the long-term.

*Long-term techniques:*

- empowerment (see Key Terms, page 23)
- job enrichment
- delegation
- team-working

Long-term motivation is important in today's competitive business environment. It can be difficult to achieve and may require a significant investment by the business.

The technique used in any given circumstances will depend upon a number of factors such as:

- *The costs involved* – for many firms this might be the determining factor. If profit margins are slim (and shareholders dissatisfied) managers may not be able to offer bonuses or piece-rate pay. They may not have funds for the training to allow implementation of a policy of delegation. Managers may find themselves in conflict with shareholders who fear that their dividends will be reduced.
- *The attitude of the management team* – some managers have a strong autocratic streak and relish being in control. Thus, they may not implement motivational techniques which would result in subordinates having greater influence over their working lives. They will be more likely to focus upon pay as a motivator.
- *The training given to the management team* – have managers received training in the theory of motivation? If they understand why their employees work, they will be more likely to apply appropriate motivational techniques. In these circumstances they may be less likely to rely solely on financial forms of motivation.
- *The skill level of the workforce* – some techniques of motivation, notably delegation, job enrichment and job rotation may require substantial employee training before they can be implemented. It would be impossible to offer employees the chance to plan their own work, take their own decisions and to carry out a number of roles as part of a multi-skilled team without substantial training.
- *The public's perception of the business* – some organisations may engage in techniques such as delegation and empowerment to project a positive corporate image. It is hoped that this will enhance company sales and assist in attracting high quality employees.
- *The effectiveness of communication* – both within and outside the business. If a business has effective two-way communication it is more likely to implement techniques such as quality circles or team-working. Firms with poor communication may rely more on piece-rate pay and job rotation.

**PROGRESS CHECK**

**Analyse the factors which might influence how a firm attempts to motivate its employees.**

# Motivating successfully

FACT FILE

The Rover Group offers many of its employees the opportunity to take part in a generous car leasing scheme which allows them to have a new car every 2 years. Under the leasing arrangements employees can lease a Rover 214Si for around £140 a month.

All organisations want their workforces to be as productive as possible. A highly motivated workforce is likely to be efficient at enhancing a business's competitive position. Managers need to consider a number of points if an organisation is to succeed in motivating its staff.

1 Being aware of what motivates individuals and ensuring that they are rewarded and recognised appropriately is crucial. However, considerable research and planning is necessary before it is possible to implement a new system intended to motivate. Schemes must be designed to meet the needs of the workforce in question, not merely 'borrowed' from other businesses.
2 Encouraging and developing the 'right' corporate culture within the organisation is central to motivation. The correct culture will vary according to circumstances, but may be customer-orientated and entrepreneurial. Creating a culture which offers employees increased authority and the opportunity to play a greater role is likely to increase their level of motivation.
3 The chosen system of motivation must be suitable for the circumstances of the organisation. Thus, job rotation may be difficult to implement if employees require high skill levels to carry out their duties. An important element is to design jobs to allow employees to meet as many of their individual needs as possible.
4 A firm must recognise that a given system of motivation will not last forever. As business cultures and society change, so new techniques will be required. For example, rising standards of living may have reduced the power of money as a motivator. Equally, increasing levels of education mean that businesses need to offer employees more challenging tasks to stimulate them.

## Measuring levels of motivation

An interesting question to consider is *how* a firm knows when it has motivated its workforce successfully. A number of indicators can provide evidence:

- It is likely that the rate of **labour turnover** will diminish in an organisation with highly motivated employees. Similarly, it is probable that the incidence of **industrial disputes** will lessen. Motivated workers are less likely to strike or take other forms of industrial action.
- Labour **productivity** should rise and businesses can reasonably expect a fall in wage costs per unit of production.
- Businesses which motivate employees successfully are likely to attract increased numbers of **applications for employment**. The quality of those applicants may also be higher.

# Disadvantages of motivational schemes

Businesses can suffer disadvantages from implementing policies designed to motivate – even if they are successful. The costs can be substantial, whether in the form of performance-related pay, additional training for managers and shop-floor workers or costs of hiring consultants.

KEY POINTS

Higher levels of motivation are likely to lead to:

- greater productivity
- better quality
- lower labour turnover
- less absenteeism.

FACT FILE

Waiters, chefs, receptionists and maids are among the least satisfied members of the workforce. This is probably not surprising given that they are four times more likely to get the sack than the average employee; 6% were sacked in the 12 months of the study (see source below). More than 40% walk out each year (well above the average of 1 in 7). Also leisure and tourism is one of the areas of highest injuries with 5.6 injuries for every 100 employees. 12% of hotel and restaurant staff work more than 48 hours a week.
*Source: Workplace–employee relations survey, Financial Times 24.09.99*

FACT FILE

Larry Durham, 56, a highly successful American entrepreneur, opted to continue working even though he received £109 million as a result of selling his school bus business. Mr Durham continued to manage the business for its new owners, National Express.

NUMERICAL INVESTIGATION

| MANUFACTURER | PLANT | PRODUCTIVITY PER EMPLOYEE (1998) |
|---|---|---|
| Nissan | Sunderland | 105 |
| Volkswagen | Navarra | 76 |
| GM | Elsenach | 76 |
| Fiat | Melfi | 73 |
| Rover Group | Longbridge | 30 |

**Table 3.2** Productivity in the car industry. *Source: The Independent, 18 August 1999*

a Nissan produced 288,838 vehicles in 1998. How many employees did it have?
b How much more productive is an average worker at Nissan's Sunderland plant compared to Rover's Longbridge plant?
c To what extent could the differences in productivity be due to motivation?

It is also important to remember that motivation does not, in itself, guarantee greater productivity. In order to improve their performance employees must also have the right skills and equipment.

PROGRESS CHECK

To what extent is the motivation of employees under the control of managers?

## How useful are the theories of motivation?

As well as understanding the theories of motivation you must be able to assess the *value* of the theories, especially their relevance to particular circumstances. An example is given below.

Different individuals are motivated by different factors – it depends on the needs they hope to fulfil through working. Thus, someone who lives alone might need to fulfil social needs from working, whilst a highly qualified professional may seek achievement and recognition. Thus, any one theory may have limited power in relation to a broad and diverse group of people. Because of this, it is unlikely that a single theory will be completely successful in explaining levels of motivation in all circumstances. Thus, Taylor's writing might explain a lack of motivation caused by inadequate pay. For many people, job insecurity has a bearing on motivation, which can be explained through the writings of Maslow.

It may appear puzzling that there are so many theories of motivation, many of which are contradictory. However, each theory should be evaluated in the context of the time in which it was written. Thus, Taylor's work emphasised the importance of money as a motivator. This was at the end of the nineteenth century when standards of living were low; thus, most people worked for money and this need was reinforced by the absence of any system of social security. Today, many employees take an adequate wage for granted and seek to fulfil other, more personal needs, through employment.

The various theories all combine to increase our understanding and perspective of employee motivation. They may not all be relevant to a particular situation but each has something to offer in different scenarios. If nothing else, the study of motivational theories should make managers think about the importance of a motivated workforce and the different ways in which employees might be motivated. The theorists do, at least, provide a range of options and approaches.

FF

FACT FILE

Cell production separates a production line into a number of units. Cells contribute to the overall product by completing a significant and distinct part of the production process.

PROGRESS CHECK

## Questions

1 Assess the usefulness of motivational theories to managers.
2 Many managers have never even heard of motivational theorists. Does this suggest the theories have no place in the modern business world?

# *Team-working*

There has been a major trend in businesses towards team-working over recent years. It is a major component of the so-called Japanese approach to production and its benefits have been extolled by major companies such as Honda, John Lewis, Toshiba and Vauxhall Motors.

**Anyone who has been part of a strong team – for however short a period – will recognise it as one of the great experiences of their life. It is not a matter of good relationships or linked friendships, some individuals might be quite cool towards one another. It is the sense that the whole group is aiming in the same direction, towards common objectives to which they are all deeply committed; a sense that there is nothing they cannot achieve.**

***Source: Taylor and Vigars, 1993***

Team-working occurs when a business breaks down its production processes into large units instead of relying upon the use of the division of labour. Introducing a production system based on teams is likely to represent major change for any business and will require thorough preparation. It cannot happen overnight.

## Creating the 'right' culture for team-working

It is unlikely that team-working will be implemented as a strategy on its own. Other elements of the Japanese approach are likely to be introduced simultaneously, or may have already been implemented. Team-working might be accompanied by:

- **cell production**
- quality circles or kaizen groups (see page 27)

- delayering (see page 58)
- delegation (see page 23)
- empowerment (see page 46).

### Encouraging participation

Shop-floor employees will need encouragement to offer their views and play a role in decision-making. Many of the employees who are asked to become active team members may have spent their entire working life performing relatively simple tasks. Encouraging participation can be very difficult, and certainly will take time to achieve. Perhaps the most important factor is to create the right type of organisational culture. This can be established and encouraged by a democratic form of leadership, and effective two-way communication.

## Implementing team-working

Team-working is more likely to be successful if employees are involved in the decision to implement it in the first place. It is simplistic for businesses to state that they are going to 'build teams' perhaps as a result of a day's training at a local hotel! Team-building should be a natural development within the organisation and must be regarded by all as the most effective structure to achieve the organisation's strategic objectives.

People in teams will only contribute to achieving team objectives when they have been part of the process that created those objectives – goals cannot be imposed upon teams from outside. Thus, the organisation needs to involve shop-floor employees in setting objectives and targets so that they feel some ownership. Members of modern teams expect to be consulted, collaborated with and supported. Working in a team helps members to feel valued and important as a person, and offers supportive relationships with other team members.

It is difficult for employees to contribute, particularly to a large organisation: they have difficulty in being heard and making an impact. It can be a struggle for employees to achieve recognition and to feel valued by their peers and managers. Breaking the workforce down into small teams can help to achieve these things.

## Training for team-working

Team-working cannot be implemented without preparing employees to fulfil a more challenging role within the organisation. Team-working requires that shop-floor employees are multi-skilled. This enables them to carry out a number of functions within the group, offering advantages to the team as well as to the organisation. These benefits include the factors listed below:

- Absences owing to holidays and illness can easily be covered.
- Jobs can be rotated as team members switch between tasks.
- Unbalanced patterns of work can be managed effectively if team members can switch smoothly between tasks.

- Team members can contribute more fully to team decisions, encouraging and facilitating empowerment.

It is likely that a substantial amount of training will be required, depending upon the degree of change involved in the move to a team-based culture. Managers, as well as shop-floor employees, will require training in order to adapt to their new roles. The company will probably incur significant direct costs in the training as well as disruption to existing operations. New staff may need to be recruited and existing ones offered early retirement (or perhaps redundancy) if they do not figure in the new scheme of things.

Teams need some direction if they are to succeed. Managers must act as coaches and facilitators to help the team develop and prosper.

**KEY POINTS**

Teams are more likely to be successful if:

- the goals are clear
- team members are well trained
- managers act as facilitators
- the organisational culture encourages co-operation
- employees are involved in the process of creating their teams.

**PROGRESS CHECK**

## Questions

1. To what extent might it be easier to implement team-working within a large-scale organisation?
2. What steps might the managers of an organisation need to take to change its culture before implementing team-working?

**FACT FILE**

A 1998 survey conducted by the Institute of Management showed that 52% of managers feared that restructuring for reasons such as developing team structures had resulted in a loss of valuable skills and experience. The equivalent figure for the previous year was 45%.

# An assessment of team-working

## The downside

Conventional wisdom has it that team-working is a good thing. However, an alternative view can be proposed. Teamworking may prove to be a fad, abandoned as businesses implement newer philosophies and techniques. It can also be argued that it is not applicable in all circumstances and that wise managers would compare carefully the costs against the expected benefits.

Conflict is a potential disadvantage from team-working and a powerful argument for maintaining other structures. It is possible to argue that conflict is inevitable within any team; in fact 'positive discontent' may help to stimulate innovation and continuous improvement. However, conflict needs to be managed. If not, it can become destructive to teams and to individuals, meaning that it is more difficult to achieve organisational goals.

We have seen that the move towards team-based structures is frequently accompanied by delayering within the organisation. This often results in early retirement or redundancy of middle managers, many of whom might have substantial experience of the business and the industry. Many firms are recognising that this approach has significant drawbacks. The loss of large numbers of experienced employees can mean that the organisation does not possess the necessary knowledge or skills to perform its functions effectively. Thus, knowledge management has become an important part of implementing teams.

Teams are not necessarily the answer to improving organisational performance. Businesses need to analyse the actual work to be completed before they take the decision to form a team or teams. It may be that the work in question is creative or simplistic and would be best completed by an individual.

FACT FILE

DEC was the US's second largest computer manufacturer. In 1997, the company disbanded its team structure. Workers in function teams (such as marketing) and product-line teams had spent hours attempting to reach agreement. The situation was worsened as many employees were members of both types of team and could not satisfy both team leaders. Problems that should have been resolved by the teams were pushed up the hierarchy for senior managers to decide.

## The pluses

The benefits of team-working are apparent and aired frequently. The advocates of team-working present a number of arguments in support of their case.

The technique of teamworking offers shop-floor employees the opportunity to fulfil the higher needs as identified by Maslow, thereby improving quality and productivity. Because employees are better motivated, they are less likely to leave the company; recruitment and retraining costs are likely to be reduced. These factors should have a significant effect in lowering overall costs and enhancing the business's profitability.

Team-working makes fuller use of the talents of the entire workforce, for example allowing those closest to problems to suggest and implement solutions. It allows individuals to complement each other's strengths and weaknesses creating a more effective and productive unit, as well as a more positive working environment.

Team-working can reduce management costs when accompanied by a delayering of the organisation. The removal of a number of middle managers is likely to cut the corporate wage bill substantially.

**A good team is a great place to be, exciting, stimulating, supportive, successful. A bad team is horrible, a sort of human prison.**

***Source: Charles Handy, Inside Organisations 1990***

PROGRESS CHECK

To what extent should UK firms make more use of more team-working?

# *Empowerment*

Empowerment can be an integral part of team-working, but this is not necessarily the case. Empowerment could be described as the modern form of delegation whereby employees are given greater control over their working lives. It gives employees the opportunity to decide how to carry out their duties and how to organise their working day. They have the opportunity to decide what to do when and how to do it.

Empowerment is based on the theories put forward by the neo-Human Relations School of thought. It is based on the premise that employees want to work, seek responsibility and enjoy the opportunity to achieve and receive recognition. It is likely to be implemented by managers who take a Theory Y view of leadership.

## The benefits of empowerment

Empowering the workforce has many implications for a business. Empowerment may result in a diminishing need for middle managers, leading to a delayered organisational structure with fewer levels of hierarchy. This can result in costly redundancies and damaged morale. The actual process of delayering can be harmful as insecurity becomes common amongst the management team. Even once the process is complete, this insecurity is unlikely to disappear. Those managers who remain may fear further cuts.

FACT FILE

Research conducted into the activities of 100 UK companies revealed that in those companies which implemented extensive policies of empowerment, increases in sales revenue of 30%, increases in return on capital of at least 12%, and increases in profit per employee of more than £5000 were reported as a consequence of this decision.

Empowerment can make the working lives of employees more interesting – it offers opportunities to meet a number of individual needs. Employees take on new responsibilities, can grow and develop as they are given greater authority, the chance to take on new roles and to acquire and develop new skills. In most circumstances this development can be expected, at least in the long-term, to have a positive impact upon productivity.

The role of supervisors can change as they increasingly adopt the role of a facilitator, encouraging and developing the team. It is probable that supervisors will not be a part of the hierarchy, but will play the role of 'team coach' – encouraging the setting and achievement of targets, developing a multi-skilled team and ensuring that people are confident and competent in their new roles.

Empowered workers can generate new methods of working as they bring a new perspective to decision-making. They may spend a part of their working lives considering the problems they face and proposing solutions. This might represent the most fundamental change in their working lives and highlight the degree of control they possess. This change in role can go further. Many empowered teams take a key role in recruiting and selecting new employees, replacing some of the functions of a personnel department.

KEY POINTS

Empowerment is more likely to occur when:

- managers have a Theory Y approach
- the culture of the organisation encourages delegation
- employees welcome authority and accept responsibility.

Empowerment is more likely to be successful if:

- it is not perceived simply as a means of reducing the number of managers
- care is taken to ensure that the organisation retains sufficient experienced employees
- it is integrated fully within the culture of the organisation
- thought is given to what is expected of junior employees and training is provided
- senior managers retain sufficient oversight of empowered workers to minimise risk.

Empowerment can help a business meet regional differences in patterns of demand by allowing local employees to take decisions, rather than impose a national view on the operation of the business. This can overcome many of the problems faced by a management team that is geographically remote.

As with all other techniques of managing people, empowerment has advantages and disadvantages. Undoubtedly, it will work better in some circumstances than in others. For a workforce used to some degree of delegation and possessing some of the necessary skills, a move to empowerment might not be too great a shock. For employees used to autocratic management and a traditional role culture, the change might be considerable. In the latter case, if the policy is to succeed, some time and resources will need to be devoted to preparation.

It may be that the real benefits of empowerment can only be seen in the long-term. In the short-term, disruption, uncertainty and adverse effects of redundancy and retirement may detract from organisational performance. Empowerment represents an investment that will not generate a quick return.

In some cases firms have used the term empowerment when, in fact, all they have been doing is giving employees additional tasks. Not surprisingly, then, some employees are very suspicious of empowerment believing that it often involves exploitation. Empowerment is meant to be liberating for employees – to give them greater control over their working lives.

PROGRESS CHECK

## Questions

1 Discuss the possible benefits of empowerment to a firm.
2 Do you think 'empowerment' is just another word for 'delegation'? Justify your answer.
3 Is empowerment a form of exploitation?

# *Summary chart*

**Figure 3.1** Key elements in motivation, team-working and empowerment

# Approaching exam questions: Motivation, team-working and empowerment

## 'Changes in society have meant that new techniques are needed to motivate employees successfully. The views of writers such as Taylor, therefore, have little or no relevance in modern businesses.' Critically analyse this statement.

**(40 marks)**

This question requires some considerable interpretation. One key to it is an appreciation that Taylor's theory was based on the premise that money is the sole motivator. This might represent a good starting point. As with most other essays, it is important to provide evidence supporting the statement as well as opposing it.

Some important arguments to consider include the following:

- Many businesses operate around the globe and the needs at work of many employees might be met through financial factors.
- A *range* of factors motivate people and those identified by Taylor may still have relevance.
- Changing living standards have meant that factors other than money have become important motivators.
- Factors such as technology, education and the changing nature of work have meant that methods of motivating people have changed.

Any judgement on this statement needs careful thought. A worthwhile approach might be to consider circumstances in which the views in the statement might be true and those in which it may not. The central premise should be that there is no simple answer.

## Mid European Airlines operate in the fiercely competitive market for international air travel. Douglas Haig, the chief executive has stated that it is impossible for any firm to compete in the air travel market without adopting a policy of empowerment. Discuss the reasoning that may lie behind this view.

**(40 marks)**

As with most essays in this book, the question appears to relate *solely* to the people module of the syllabus, but this is not the case. You should be prepared to introduce material from other areas of the syllabus. You will not be penalised for taking this approach – indeed it is advisable to view any essay as a business studies essay, not as a question on a single part of the syllabus.

This essay would require some discussion of the benefits that a policy of empowerment may bring. The candidate should cover the positive effects of empowerment and relate these to the competitive position of the business. Thus, productivity and costs, problem-solving and staffing levels could be important issues in responding to this question.

However, other factors are also important – quality of management, exchange rates, technical advances and so on ... Empowerment alone will not make a firm competitive.

## 'Our lack of understanding of the causes of human behaviour is shown by the varying approaches to motivation used by businesses.' Discuss this statement.

**(40 marks)**

This question requires the balanced approach common to so many essays. It may be worth a brief consideration of the approaches firms use to motivate employees. This is the basic content of an answer to this question.

You could support the argument in the question in a number of ways. Motivation varies according to, for example, the style of leadership in a business, its culture and the personality of the leader. It is possible to support the view in the title by arguing that some of the various approaches pay little attention to the individuals who comprise the workforce and the needs they might have.

However, it is also possible to refute the argument in the question. A number of theories of motivation exist; if managers believe in different theories, they will use different motivational techniques. The 'best' managers employ techniques appropriate to the circumstances. Employees are not all the same – different factors may be necessary to motivate different individuals.

Evaluation could centre upon the fact that the question may be based on an incorrect premise – are that many approaches actually used? It may not be lack of understanding, it could be shortage of money that prevents the use of some motivational techniques, for example.

## Textbook theory sets out clear advantages to be gained from empowerment. Analyse possible reasons why a small and traditional manufacturing business may not adopt this technique of managing employees.

**(9 marks)**

This question calls for sound understanding of empowerment and an ability to apply that knowledge to the circumstances in the question. A good starting point might be a brief definition of empowerment. This convinces the examiner of your subject knowledge and helps to focus your thoughts.

Relevant points might include:

- a lack of knowledge on the part of the managers – who may be untrained
- insufficient money to pay for training shop-floor workers
- a culture that does not support the passing down of authority
- leaders who are reluctant to surrender control.

Arguments such as this would be entirely appropriate. You will note that they are the sort of arguments that could be applied to a small business with traditional values.

# Student answers: Motivation, team-working and empowerment

## Analyse the factors that might influence a business in its choice of motivational system.

**(9 marks)**

### Student answer

There are a number of ways in which businesses can motivate their workers. They can use performance-related pay systems, offer employees greater authority or use techniques such as piece-rate pay. The system a business chooses will depend upon the circumstances.

If a business has little money, it might have to use non-monetary methods to motivate its workers. If it has a lot of money then it can use monetary methods.

The technique used to motivate employees might depend upon the type of work that the business does – it could be easier in a factory.

Finally, it will depend on the views and beliefs of the senior managers – some of them may not support modern management techniques.

### *Marker's comments*

*This response is disappointing in that the student has limited subject knowledge and no discernible examination technique. The opening paragraph is entirely irrelevant. The student would have been better advised to think a little more about what the question required before starting writing. The latter part of the answer is simply a list of points with no analysis. By developing an argument around why, for example, the type of business should influence the system of motivation employed, the candidate could have written analytically and attracted higher marks.*

**Mark: Content 2/2, Application 1/4, Analysis 0/3. Total = 3**

# Evaluate the view that empowerment is merely a means of replacing costly employees with less expensive ones.

**(11 marks)**

## Student answer

In some circumstances empowerment can be regarded as a means of cutting the wage bill. Delayering of the organisation and the redundancy of middle managers often accompany empowerment. At the same time, the workforce is reorganised to allow shop-floor employees to take on the roles and duties formerly carried out by managers. This cuts expenditure on wages and can improve the profitability of the business.

However, empowerment can be an effective technique to motivate employees. It allows shop-floor employees to have greater control over their working lives and to fulfil a range of needs such as achievement and recognition. Empowerment can also offer other benefits. Employees can gain a range of skills to allow production to progress more smoothly and they can generate ideas for improvement. This can increase productivity as shop-floor employees bring a different perspective to decision-making and problem-solving.

Whether the quotation is true depends upon the objectives behind the decision and the degree of preparation. If senior managers aim for highly skilled and productive employees who have control over their work, then any reduction in the wage bill may be a beneficial side-effect. However, other more cynical, managers may focus on short-term cost reductions.

### *Marker's comments*

*This is a good quality answer, though the student may have spent too long in developing his arguments and run out of time later in the examination. However, it brings together sound subject knowledge and effective examination technique to provide a high quality response. The student has not been too ambitious and has developed the analysis fully before offering some evaluation in the final paragraph. The student wrote the answer in three paragraphs looking at each side of the argument before evaluating. This was a highly effective structure – guiding the examiner through the various elements of the answer.*

**Mark: Content 2/2, Application & Analysis 6/6, Evaluation 3/3. Total = 11**

# Analyse the implications for shop-floor employees in a large manufacturing business of the adoption of a team-working strategy.

**(9 marks)**

## Student answer

Team-working will change the working lives of the shop-floor workers in this business. These changes will be for the better. The workers can expect to be given greater responsibility for their own work and to play a bigger role in decision-making. This should improve their motivation and productivity.

Team-working will require workers to carry out a wider range of duties as they may have to provide cover for absent colleagues and to use a range of skills when business is hectic. This should reduce boredom and help employees.

Employees may also be involved in what were previously management roles – taking decisions and solving problems. This can be highly motivating for shop-floor workers as they are offered the chance to fulfil some of their higher needs or motivators.

### *Marker's comment*

*This is a sound answer with a number of pleasing features. The student has a good subject knowledge of this area of the syllabus. He or she understands some of the important interrelationships between, for example, team-working and motivation. The answer has also followed through a line of argument to show some of implications of the implementation of team-working for shop-floor employees.*

*However, the student does paint a rather rosy picture of team-working. The answer fails to mention some of the downsides – possible loss of jobs or the breaking up of established work groups.*

**Mark: Content 2/2, Application 4/4, Analysis 2/3. Total = 8**

# Evaluate the steps a business may take to motivate its workforce during a period of economic recession.

**(11 marks)**

A business can take a number of steps to improve motivation.

- It can move away from piece-rate pay towards salaries for all employees.
- It can train its managers in the latest management techniques.
- The business might assure its employees that their jobs are secure.
- The business could offer voluntary redundancy or early retirement to help reduce the labour force without making compulsory redundancies.
- It may improve working conditions or offer employees the opportunity for achievement.

The business will have to decide upon the best approaches and this will depend upon a number of factors including the style of leadership.

### *Marker's comments*

*This is a very weak answer but it is interesting in that it contains three common errors, which should be avoided at all costs. Firstly, the student did not pay attention to the scenario included in the question. The answer contains no reference to recession. Secondly, the use of bullet points in questions requiring analysis and evaluation is most unwise. Analysis and evaluation require arguments to be developed in a number of sentences. Bullet points make writing in this style very difficult.*

*The final error is the evaluation. The answer does not really contain an evaluation. The student has merely offered a line of argument that might be evaluative in the right circumstances. However, in this context it is not evaluative. Evaluation cannot be learned in this way. It is a skill – not knowledge.*

**Mark: Content 2/2, Application & Analysis 0/6, Analysis 0/3. Total = 2**

# End of section questions

1 Examine how an increase in motivation may benefit a firm.
(9 marks)

2 To what extent might a business motivate its workforce through the use of monetary rewards?
(11 marks)

3 Consider the benefits a business might expect as a consequence of motivating its employees successfully.
(11 marks)

4 To what extent can performance indicators such as the rate of labour turnover measure the level of motivation within a workforce?
(11 marks)

5 Analyse why successful motivation can be difficult to achieve in the long-term.
(9 marks)

6 Examine the reasons why a business needs to prepare thoroughly before introducing team-working.
(9 marks)

7 Discuss whether team-working can be implemented successfully without other key elements of the Japanese approach such as kaizen.
(11 marks)

8 To what extent might the costs of team-working outweigh the benefits?
(11 marks)

9 Evaluate the view that empowerment is merely a means of replacing costly employees with less expensive ones.
(11 marks)

10 Consider the likely implications for a large manufacturing business of a decision to empower its shop-floor employees.
(11 marks)

# Essays

1 'The key to successful motivation is effective two-way communication.' To what extent do you agree with this statement?
(40 marks)

2 The managing director of a major multi-national corporation has commented that empowerment is doomed to failure. 'Replacing experienced and knowledgeable middle managers with naïve shop-floor employees will always disadvantage the business.' Critically assess this view.
(40 marks)

3 Clare Wilson, Managing Director of one of Europe's largest banking and finance groups, has stated publicly that team-working requires thorough preparation if it is to have a chance of success. Discuss the importance of this issue.
(40 marks)

4 A Managing Director is reported to have commented: 'It is not surprising that businesses are keen to introduce empowered teams. Such teams offer the opportunity to persuade people to take on more responsibilities without increasing their pay or status. This cannot be in the best interests of a business'. Discuss this statement.
(40 marks)

5 'The best way to motivate workers is to pay them well and to provide them with secure employment.' Assess this view of motivation.
(40 marks)

CHAPTER 4

# The structure and culture of organisations



## Introduction

The organisational structure is the particular way in which the jobs within a firm are arranged in order for it to carry out its activities. The structure sets out the relationship between the different elements of the business, including the lines of communication and authority. Nowadays, it is common for the structure of organisations to change rapidly and regularly. This pace of change has focused attention on the ways in which businesses in the UK structure and organise themselves.

**FACT FILE**

**In January 1999, IPC magazines (publisher of *Loaded* and *Country Life*) axed 2000 jobs as part of a cost-cutting exercise. The company stated that it was attempting to bring about a more flexible, creative and entrepreneurial organisational culture.**

A principal reason for the regular change in organisational structures is the pace of *external* change which requires businesses to respond to an ever changing environment. A major example of this is delayering whereby organisations have eliminated layers of hierarchy, mainly middle managers. This move towards 'flatter' organisational structures has been prompted by competitive pressures (for example, the need to reduce costs) and by the desire to improve motivation by offering those further down the organisational structure greater authority and control over their working lives.

**KEY TERM**

**Levels of hierarchy** refer to the number of layers of authority within an organisation.

The subject of organisational culture has received much attention from the media over recent years. The goal of many businesses is to create a culture that is conducive to change itself, a responsive and flexible culture. We shall consider this topic in more detail later in this chapter.

**A well designed organisation allows managers to make the right decisions and get things done; a poorly designed structure makes it more difficult to succeed.**

## Organisational structures

Typical organisational structures that a business may adopt include:

- *Formal or traditional hierarchy* – this structure distributes decision-making throughout the business and gives all employees a clearly defined role, as well as establishing their relationship with other employees in the business. It is common for this type of organisational structure to be based upon depart-

FACT FILE

Bill Gates' Microsoft Corporation is often quoted as an example of an organisation with an informal structure. Staff have been seen discussing software problems in swimwear whilst playing volleyball!

ments and because of the dependence upon agreed procedures it can be bureaucratic.

- *Matrix structure* – this is a task-orientated structure. It puts together teams of individuals with the specialist skills necessary to complete a particular project. The aim is to allow all individuals to use their talents effectively irrespective of their position within the organisation.
- *Entrepreneurial structure* – frequently found in small businesses operating in competitive markets. A few key workers at the core of the organisation – often the owner(s) – make decisions. The business is heavily dependent upon the knowledge and skills of these key workers.
- *Informal structures* – this is where the organisation does not have an obvious structure. It is common in the case of professional practices (doctors and lawyers often work in this way, for example; they operate as a team). The professionals normally receive administrative support from others within the organisation.

So, modern organisations expect to change their structures frequently in response to external pressures. Some chief executives believe reorganisation is a permanent feature of their businesses.

## The implications of structure

The nature of an organisation's structure affects the speed of decision-making, the flexibility of the organisation, costs, the culture of the firm and its overall efficiency and effectiveness. A well designed structure enables quick decision-making and keeps costs low; information flows easily around the organisation and decisions are made by appropriate people. Badly designed organisations are often bureaucratic, slow to respond and demotivating for employees.

PROGRESS CHECK

**Explain how organisational structure could affect the competitiveness of a firm.**

## Factors determining organisational structures

When deciding upon an organisational structure business leaders will take into account a number of factors. These include:

- *The environment in which the business is operating* – fierce competitive pressures may encourage delayering in an effort to reduce costs, whilst rapid change can emphasise the need for a matrix structure so that the organisation can keep up-to-date. The matrix structure would also eliminate the possibility of inflexible hierarchies getting in the way of rapid decision-making.
- *The size of the business* – many small businesses begin with an entrepreneurial structure in which the owner plays a central role. He or she will not be able to sustain this position as the business grows and a large firm is more likely to be organised traditionally, or perhaps as a matrix.

- *The strategic objectives of the business* – an innovative and highly competitive organisation may opt for a matrix structure in order to complete tasks effectively. On the other hand, a business focusing on the quality of its design and production (as opposed to growth) may suit an entrepreneurial structure. The latter structure may be appropriate for businesses in a craft industry, for example.
- *The skills of the workforce* – the higher the level of skill that a typical employee has, the more likely it is that the business will organise along matrix or informal lines. A small group of professionals, such as management consultants or estate agents, may simply carry out their professional duties with administrative support from the organisation. Less skilled employees may respond better to a formal structure with more authority retained further up the hierarchy.
- *The culture of the organisation* – if a business has a highly innovative culture and it wishes to be a market leader selling advanced products, then it may adopt a matrix structure. This helps to minimise bureaucracy and allows teams to carry out the necessary product research and development, and market research. On the other hand, an organisation which places an emphasis on tradition (and derives its commercial success from appearing conventional) may be best suited to a formal hierarchical structure. Viewing positions rather than people as important, this structure encourages the continuance of existing policies and practices. Some high-class hotels may fall into this category.

**KEY POINTS**

A matrix structure is more likely when:

- the organisation is highly innovative;
- the environment is changing rapidly;
- the firm's activities are changing and developing rapidly;
- the employees are highly skilled;
- the tasks undertaken involve a high degree of project work.

**PROGRESS CHECK**

**Discuss the possible reasons why a firm might adopt a matrix structure.**

## Styles of leadership and organisational structure

An interesting relationship exists between leadership styles and the structure an organisation adopts. Clearly, it is possible to argue that the style a leader adopts will shape the way in which a business is structured.

Thus, a democratic leader (see page 23) who takes a Theory Y (see page 26) view of employees may opt for a matrix structure, allowing staff a high degree of authority to complete the tasks necessary to achieve the organisation's objectives. A matrix structure contains relatively few layers of hierarchy and consequently the spans of control would be broad. In certain circumstances, and depending upon the skill levels of employees, such a leader may decide upon an informal structure for the organisation.

**KEY TERM**

The **span of control** is the number of subordinates reporting directly to a manager.

A leader favouring an autocratic style of leadership and perhaps possessing a Theory X view of workers may favour either a traditional, formal structure or an entrepreneurial structure, depending upon the size of the business. Thus, a small business with this style of leader may operate an entrepreneurial structure which allows the leader a high degree of control (and subordinates relatively little authority). However, at some point the organisation may become too large and complex to be controlled in this way and the structure could gradually change to become formal and hierarchical, whilst still allowing the owner to retain a high degree of control.

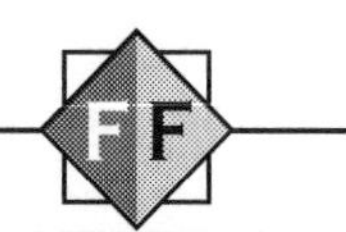

FACT FILE

Helmut Maucher, Managing Director of Nestlé, is credited with creating an organisational culture which is anti-paper, anti-bureaucratic and emphasises long-term planning.

KEY POINTS

A formal structure is more likely when:

- the managers adopt a Theory X approach
- the culture of the organisation is conservative
- the environment is relatively stable
- the task is fairly predictable.

FACT FILE

Archie Norman, Chairman of ASDA, commented favourably on the take-over of his company by the giant US retailer Wal-Mart '... culturally we are so similar it is like coming home'.

Finally, a laissez-faire leader may elect to use an informal structure as this involves minimal control over subordinates and no real structure for the business.

PROGRESS CHECK

## Questions

1 **Examine the ways in which the culture of an organisation might affect its structure.**
2 **In what ways might the structure affect the culture?**

## Is there a 'best' structure?

The preceding section should have made it clear that there is no one structure which is appropriate for all organisations, or even for one organisation throughout its existence. It is tempting to criticise traditional, formal structures for being old-fashioned, costly and having little relevance to modern businesses. As we have seen, this is not the case. There are scenarios and circumstances in which such a structure would be appropriate and effective. Similar arguments can be put forward for matrix, entrepreneurial or informal structures.

We do, however, tend to think of an organisation operating a single structure. It may be that large businesses, in fact, operate more than one structure, reflecting the different needs of various areas of the organisation. Thus a large firm may:

- operate its research and development division on an informal basis to make the most effective use of talented and highly skilled scientists
- base its administration on a traditional structure, in the expectation of achieving a high standard of work and to benefit from a consistent approach to this aspect of business
- organise its sales and marketing teams on a matrix structure and have clear targets and tasks to achieve.

All these different structures and the associated cultures could, therefore, be found within a single organisation. Dangers exist in this approach: the organisation could become difficult to co-ordinate and some divisions may begin to pursue their own objectives, different from those of the business as a whole.

So, we cannot make the judgement that a particular organisational structure is 'best'. This depends upon the circumstances. The fact that businesses change their structures so frequently shows that today's organisational structure may not be appropriate tomorrow.

# *Delayering*

Firms review their position regularly and take decisions appropriate to their circumstances. Despite the view that there is no single 'best' structure, some common approaches to organisational structures have emerged over recent years. One approach which has received a great deal of media publicity is delayering – or reducing the number of levels of hierarchy within an organisation.

PROGRESS CHECK

## Questions

1 What organisational structures would you consider appropriate in the following circumstances?
- the design team for a fashion house
- the British Embassy in Paris
- a firm developing state-of-the-art computer software
- a small, newly formed business with a dynamic and forceful managing director
- the Norfolk police force
- a business which regularly requires rapid decisions for commercial success.

You should provide a justification for each of your decisions, explaining why your chosen structure would be most appropriate to the circumstances.

2 Explain why the structure of an organisation might be an important factor determining the success of a business.

FACT FILE

In the 1970s, prior to any delayering, General Motors, the American motor manufacturer, had 29 layers of hierarchy within its organisational structure.

The growing intensity of competition in international markets, and particularly from companies in the Far East, has forced businesses to reduce their costs. Delayering the business is one way in which costs have been lowered. Traditionally, reductions in employment to reduce costs and improve competitiveness have resulted in the loss of jobs on the shop floor. However, increasing commercial pressures to lower costs and the development of management theories which emphasise the benefits from techniques such as delegation, empowerment and team-working have combined to put the jobs of middle managers in jeopardy. One result of this process has been the creation of 'flatter' organisations which some describe as 'leaner and more responsive'.

## Advantages of delayering

- Reduces costs by removing a number of expensive middle managers.
- Can improve responsiveness by bringing senior managers and customers closer together.
- Can motivate employees lower down in the organisation by giving them greater responsibility and control over their working lives.
- Communication may improve as there are less levels of hierarchy for a message to pass through.
- It can produce good ideas from a new perspective as shop floor employees take some decisions.

## Disadvantages of delayering

- Delayering can reduce organisational performance as valuable knowledge and experience may be lost.
- Morale and motivation may suffer because employees feel insecure.

KEY POINTS

Delayering is desirable in a firm which suffers from:

- slow decision-making
- slow communication from top to bottom of the organisation
- high management costs as a high percentage of turnover
- underutilised employees.

In addition, employees must have the skills to take on extra work.

FACT FILE

Barclays Bank shed 6000 staff (10% of its UK employees) in May 1999 at an immediate cost of £400 million, but in the hope of saving £200 million annually. Many of the employees leaving the bank were middle managers.

- Some businesses may use the excuse of delayering to make a large number of employees redundant.
- Because delayering means employees have to take on new roles within the organisation, extensive (and expensive) retraining may be required.
- Delayering can lead to intolerable workloads and high levels of stress amongst employees.

PROGRESS CHECK

**Consider the possible consequences for an organisation of delayering.**

## Does delayering work?

It is tempting to believe that every business should delayer to retain a competitive edge. It is also true that many businesses have taken the decision to flatten their structures and that observers of business expect this trend to continue into the twenty-first century.

However, as the section above highlights, there are distinct advantages and disadvantages. If delayering is to succeed in improving the performance of the business a number of factors need to be considered:

- Why is delayering being proposed? There is some evidence that senior managers propose and enact delayering to give them greater control over the organisation. Middle managers can sometimes dilute the degree of control exercised by senior managers and directors. The critical question to ask is whether the process of delayering will help the business to achieve its corporate objectives. If the answer is no, then other policies and procedures may prove more effective.
- Managing the process of delayering is vital if the policy is to be successful. If managers are to be made redundant, the selection process should be fair and the criteria should be made public. Consultation is important and support is necessary for those who lose their jobs, as well as those who remain. Demoted employees have to be handled sensitively and offered the opportunity to retrain – if only to relearn 'old' skills. It is important to reduce the level of insecurity amongst those managers who remain.
- Reorganisation is an essential partner of delayering. Firms cannot just remove a layer of the hierarchy and not plan who is to take on the responsibilities of the missing layer. This process of reorganisation requires that job specifications are redrawn and retraining is provided for employees above and below the layer removed. It is important to avoid damaging organisational performance by overloading employees.
- Flattening the organisation structure can be expensive. Making people redundant is not always a cheap option (especially if the firm wishes to retain a positive corporate image). The whole process is likely to make heavy demands upon the personnel department – if the firm has one. In addition, the company's performance may dip during the period of reorganisation as people adjust to their new roles.

- The organisation may need to come to terms with a new culture in which employees cannot expect a job for life and in which they have a lower level of loyalty to the business than might previously have been the case. This may manifest itself in a higher level of labour turnover and a significant increase in recruitment costs.

KEY POINTS

Delayering is more likely to be effective if:

- employees understand the need for it
- unions and employees are involved in the process
- there are significant cost savings
- the organisation becomes more flexible as a result
- employees do not become too overloaded.

PROGRESS CHECK

**A major UK bank has announced an extensive restructuring programme, involving delayering. Consider the possible effects of this on the firm's performance.**

## Delayering and the role of the manager

Working in a delayered organisation places different demands upon managers at all levels within the business. For senior managers, their span of control is likely to widen significantly and they may take direct responsibility for a substantial part of the organisation. They will have more contact with those further down the organisational structure and considerable demands may be placed on their communication skills. They will have to be comfortable with delegating authority as they will be unable to play a prominent part in the entire area for which they have responsibility.

KEY POINTS

Delayering is more likely to improve organisational performance if:

- It fits in with agreed corporate objectives;
- It is carefully planned in advance;
- It is conducted sensitively to avoid damaging employee morale;
- Senior managers allocate sufficient resources to the process.

Middle managers will have disappeared – to some extent at least. In many delayered organisations 'facilitators' or team leaders replace them. This role varies according to the type of business and the structure adopted. Whether firms have facilitators or team leaders, their roles have some common features:

- The role focuses on *supporting* colleagues as opposed to exercising authority.
- Team leaders or facilitators encourage all employees to play a part in *decision-making* to make the best use of the skills and knowledge available to the business.
- This role may involve negotiating *targets* for groups of workers and encouraging colleagues in the achievement of these targets.
- A key element of this role is to *develop colleagues* and to improve their performance.

PROGRESS CHECK

**Should managers welcome delayering?**

In conclusion, it is easy to argue that the process of delayering may damage the business in the short-term whilst offering substantial long-term benefits. This may be too simplistic, although depending upon circumstances it could be the case. It is important to be aware that flattening the organisational structure can have significant negative effects on a firm if it is not managed well. Many firms have suffered the consequences of rushing into a policy of delayering without adequate planning and with insufficient resources.

KEY TERMS

**Centralisation**
places decision-making powers firmly in the hands of senior personnel (often at head office).

**Decentralisation**
is the opposite – giving decision-making powers to those at lower levels in the organisation and employees in branch offices and other locations.

PROGRESS CHECK

Should the stakeholders of a firm oppose delayering?

# *Centralisation and decentralisation*

In a **decentralised organisation** there will be a high level of delegation giving those lower down the organisational structure a fair degree of authority. In contrast, a **centralised organisation** retains most authority and control in the hands of senior managers at the centre of the organisation.

## Why decentralise?

Decentralisation offers a number of benefits to a business, many of which might be expected to improve its competitive performance.

It provides subordinates with the opportunity to fulfil needs such as achievement and recognition through working. This should improve motivation and reduce the business's costs by, for example, reducing the rate of labour turnover.

It reduces the workload on senior managers allowing them to focus on strategic (rather than operational) issues. At the same time, it offers junior managers an opportunity to develop their skills in preparation for a more senior position. Many junior employees in the organisation may have better understanding of operational matters and delegation may allow them to use their skills and understanding to good effect.

**'Surround yourself with the best people you can find, delegate authority and don't interfere.' – Ronald Reagan (Former US President)**

### Factors for successful decentralisation

For decentralisation to have a greater chance of success, a business will require a number of pre-existing characteristics:

- a management team with strong Theory Y views of their employees and the necessary skills (especially in relation to communication) to operate this style of leadership
- a corporate commitment to training – firms cannot just decide to decentralise and leave employees to cope with new roles and greater authority
- a culture that is open, flexible and committed to completing tasks or projects
- effective channels for two-way communication and a positive goal-orientated environment that is conducive to delegation
- few layers of hierarchy – it may be that a matrix structure is the most appropriate for a firm practising a high degree of decentralisation

- a strong and unambiguous corporate identity and commitment to agreed goals that are unlikely to be damaged by spreading authority throughout the organisation. If this is not the case then elements within the organisation may start pulling in different directions.

FACT FILE

International food producer, Heinz, has abandoned decentralisation and created a new organisational structure based on its product ranges. The company will operate six core categories (including ketchup and sauces!) following its £450 million restructuring.

PROGRESS CHECK

## Questions

1. **Distinguish between decentralisation and delayering. Should decentralisation accompany a policy of delayering?**
2. **Examine the characteristics of a business that may not be suited to a policy of decentralisation.**

# *Organisational cultures*

Organisational cultures are neither static nor permanent. They develop over time in response to many factors. Many different types of organisational culture exist. Various writers have provided frameworks for classifying cultures. The list below is based on the writing of Charles Handy with a single addition.

- A **traditional** or **role culture** is typical of a conventional firm which operates in a bureaucratic manner and places value on conventional behaviour. Employees are expected to follow the rules and emphasis is given to hierarchy and roles within the organisation.
- A **person-orientated** culture is characterised by focusing on fulfilling the needs of individuals within an organisation. It allows individuals freedom to shape their jobs and operate with a degree of independence.
- **Task cultures** focus on solving problems. Expert teams or groups are assembled to tackle particular problems or to complete projects. This culture attaches importance to expertise, flexibility and creativity.
- A **power culture** places considerable emphasis on personal charisma and risk-taking. It disregards procedures and values entrepreneurship.
- A **change culture** can be highly valued in some circumstances. It refers to a flexible, responsive organisation capable of adapting effectively and quickly to external stimuli.

KEY POINTS

Decentralisation may be an inappropriate strategy (i.e. centralisation may be preferable) when:

- a business is facing a period of crisis and tough decisions need to be made quickly;
- an unhealthy degree of rivalry exists between divisions or departments within the organisation;
- a traditional, bureaucratic culture exists, placing more emphasis on posts rather than people;
- the leader of the business has a strong personality and equates leadership with control.

PROGRESS CHECK

**Explain how the culture of an organisation might affect managers' decisions.**

## Culture and organisational structures

There is a strong interrelationship between the prevailing culture within an organisation and the structure of the organisation. It is too simple to say that culture shapes the structure employed, or that the structure of the organisation determines its culture; the two co-exist and influence one another. Certain cultures and structures tend to go hand-in-hand.

**FACT FILE**

In 1998, SmithKline Beecham drew up a statement of its core values which centred on customers, innovation, integrity, people and performance. These were intended to bring together the US and UK sides of the business and ensure that behaviour was consistent throughout the business. 'Every organisation has a culture. A culture happens either by accident or design ... and we are going to design ours' said the firm's Chief Executive.

**FACT FILE**

ING is a Dutch financial firm with over 80,000 staff which operates in more than 60 countries. To ensure that employees in these different countries make decisions in the same way, the firm uses CD-Rom and Internet technology for training. Employees work through a number of ethical problems using the CD-Rom and discuss how they would react with their colleagues; they then watch the Board's of Directors' response which highlights the underlying business principles they want adopted. Feedback can also be received via the company's website.

### Traditional culture – hierarchical structure

A traditional or role culture is likely to exist in a conventional or hierarchical organisational structure. The emphasis that this culture places on bureaucracy and convention would be appropriate in an organisation that considers roles and hierarchy to be important. Indeed such a structure would foster a role culture.

### Task culture – matrix structure

An organisation with a matrix structure may be expected to have a task culture. Both place emphasis on combining individuals into teams to tackle projects or to solve problems. Strong formal hierarchies do not allow the flexibility and lack of role specialisation which this culture demands if it is to thrive.

### Person-orientated culture – informal structure

A person-orientated culture could reasonably be expected to co-exist with an informal organisational structure. Informal structures do not have a high degree of organisation beyond providing administrative support for what are often professional groups of people such as barristers or accountants. Many professional groups would consider appropriate a culture which encourages people to utilise their skills and talents independently in the pursuit of the organisation's objectives. Indeed, being constrained by an organisational structure to carry out a limited range of tasks may not make the most effective use of highly trained and motivated employees.

### Power culture – entrepreneurial structure

A power culture is likely to evolve within an organisation with an entrepreneurial structure. This may be a relatively small business, possibly operating within a rapidly changing (often highly technical) market. Such an organisation may benefit from a high degree of centralisation and strong leadership allied to decisiveness. A charismatic individual as a leader will encourage the development of this type of culture.

Whilst organisational structures do play an important role in determining the culture of an organisation (and vice-versa), other factors also play a part. The style of leadership, the background and level of skills of the workforce, the history of the organisation and the nature of its market will also shape the culture to some extent.

**PROGRESS CHECK**

**Outline the factors which might determine the culture of an organisation.**

## Can cultures be changed?

The idea of changing corporate culture has attracted a great deal of attention in management circles. Many management teams have bemoaned that their prevailing culture is inappropriate and often obstructive to change. For example, an organisation which has a role culture with closely defined and highly specialised jobs may find it difficult to operate in a fiercely competitive market, requiring adaptability and a high degree of creativity from employees.

Winning over people is more important in creating a change culture than implementing new structures or introducing new policies.

If a culture is strongly embedded within the organisation, it may prove very difficult to change. A number of factors determine how strong an organisation's culture may be.

- *The rate of labour turnover* – if a business experiences a low level of labour turnover then the prevailing culture is likely to be reinforced. Change is easier to effect when large numbers of new employees enter the business regularly.
- *The nature and background of the workforce* – the culture of some groups of employees develops over a number of years (perhaps in difficult and testing circumstances). In situations such as this, the culture may prove almost impossible to change. The culture of workers in many of the UK's former mining communities was strongly embedded, having evolved over a number of generations.
- *The extent to which structure reinforces culture* – a role culture may be difficult to change if emphasis is given to hierarchy and position. It may be necessary to change the structure to change the culture.
- *Informal communication* – if the operation of the business allows employees the opportunity to communicate informally, during regular tea breaks for example, the existing culture is likely to be reinforced.

It is doubtful whether a culture can be changed significantly in the short-term. A key factor may be the extent to which the aspects discusssed above can be manipulated by management action. Changing an organisation's culture may require a structural reorganisation, recruitment and perhaps implementation of new policies such as empowerment. It is not just the shop floor employees who have to change, but also the management team; the existing culture may be firmly embedded there too!

Firms may change one inappropriate culture for another that becomes equally inappropriate in a short space of time. This can happen to organisations that operate within a volatile environment. Managers may seek to inculcate a change culture which is flexible, responsive and less likely to become unsuitable in the modern world of business.

When undertaking a culture change success should not be expected in the short-term: changing an organisation's culture takes time.

**PROGRESS CHECK**

**To what extent can the culture of an organisation be changed?**

## Culture and competitiveness

One school of thought argues that a successful business is one which focuses on the behaviour of employees. The argument is that, if employees have the right attitudes

**FACT FILE**

Johnson and Johnson's credo records the firm's central beliefs and the ways it wants to do business. At regular intervals managers' performances are measured, not only in terms of their ability to deliver results, but also their observed commitment to the credo. If managers achieve their targets without sticking to the principles of the credo this is as bad as not hitting the targets at all.

**FACT FILE**

Multinational oil and gas explorers Enterprise Oil and Lasmo called off their planned merger in March 1999, citing cultural differences as a major reason for deciding to remain separate.

**KEY POINTS**

Changing an organisation's culture is easier if:

- Employees participate in the change rather than having it imposed upon them;
- Managers reward appropriate behaviour by employees.
- The organisation's structure is changed to suit the new culture;
- Employees become used to change and accept that no culture is permanent.

**FACT FILE**

A recent survey revealed that British managers are noted for their lack of humour. Despite attempts to create a more relaxed culture (through 'dress down' days for example) in general British business remains formal.

**KEY POINTS**

Organisational culture is important to businesses because:

- Techniques such as delayering and empowerment have increased the importance of employee attitudes and behaviour to businesses;
- Customer service is an important competitive factor for many businesses and this depends upon employee attitudes and behaviour.
- The business environment is changing ever more rapidly and, increasingly, firms need a culture which allows them to be responsive to their environment.

and behave in the desired manner, the business will flourish. Thus, *managing* the corporate culture is believed by many leaders to be a vital element of commercial success.

To some extent this argument might be true. For most businesses, particularly those in a changing environment, developing the appropriate culture is beneficial. It can also enhance the competitiveness of an organisation. Having an appropriate culture may limit conflict and lessen the possibility of industrial disputes. It may (in the long-term) reduce labour turnover and improve employee motivation, once resistance to the change in culture has been overcome. Changing the culture of an organisation can make the business more innovative, encouraging the development of new, modern products. All of these factors should help a business to improve its competitive performance.

However, other factors also influence a business's competitiveness. Factors such as exchange rates, interest rates and government economic policies are important determinants of competitiveness. Similarly, the actions of competitors (introducing new, advanced products for example) will affect the competitiveness of firms. Finally, the public's perception of the business (possibly shaped by the actions of pressure groups) will also play a role in determining the competitiveness of a business.

Any judgement on the importance of culture in determining a business's competitiveness has to take into account that there are many other important factors, some of which are beyond the control of the management team. Whilst changing culture may improve the internal performance of a business, the environment in which it operates can alter, having an adverse impact upon the organisation's competitiveness. Culture can, however, determine how effectively the business responds to external change.

**PROGRESS CHECK**

## Questions

1. List six factors that may determine the culture of an organisation.
2. Draw up a list of pros and cons for attempting to change an organisation's culture.
3. What type of organisational cultures do you think the following types of leaders would encourage:
   - democratic
   - autocratic
   - paternalistic
   - laissez-faire?
4. To what extent does the competitiveness of an organisation depend on its culture?

# *Summary chart*

**Figure 4.1** Key elements in the structure and culture of organisations

# Approaching exam questions: The structure and culture of organisations

## 'Flattening the structure of the organisation should be approached with caution. In many circumstances the costs of delayering can exceed any advantages. Businesses should not assume that they would automatically benefit.' Critically analyse this statement.

**(40 marks)**

This is a slightly unusual question. It is uncommon for examination questions to be based on a quotation which, at first sight, appears to be eminently sensible! However, this should not mislead the reader. This question invites students to offer evidence *in support* of the quotation. Certainly, costs such as those resulting from redundancy may be substantial. Equally, the firm might suffer a short-term rise in costs due to disruption and dislocation.

However, this question also invites students to offer a brief critique of *the case for* delayering – the potential for empowerment and all the financial and non-financial advantages that the approach can confer on an organisation. Evaluation might centre upon issues such as the public's perception of a firm's motives for delayering and how this might affect recruitment and sales.

## 'Changing the culture of a business is a risky operation.' Discuss the risks that a firm might face and how they may be minimised.

**(40 marks)**

This question has two distinct parts to it. It is important that the answer is structured so as to cover both elements of the question.

The first section is relatively straightforward. Some discussion is required of possible risks such as:

- conflict
- demotivation
- declining productivity
- loss of competitiveness
- lessening of focus on corporate objectives.

It would be important to argue that the risks would vary according to the circumstances of the firm, how well the change was managed and so on.

The second part of the question is more challenging. The techniques used to minimise the risk involved in changing corporate culture depend on the type of firm, the strength of the culture and other factors. However, tactics such as clear communication, involving employees in the decisions and rewarding appropriate employee behaviour may be considered. Once again it is important to appreciate that there is no simple answer to such a question – as in so many cases, a useful phrase is 'it depends'.

## Paul Wagstaff, Chief Executive of R. K. Mining, a privately owned coal mine, believes that managers waste too much time worrying about changing corporate cultures. 'Our company has a strong and unchanging culture and I consider that managers should concentrate on other issues such as generating higher sales.' To what extent do you agree with Paul Wagstaff?

**(40 marks)**

An organisation's culture can undoubtedly contribute to the success of the business. A number of issues need to be considered in relation to corporate culture of any kind.

- Does it fit in with the organisation's corporate objectives?
- Is the style of leadership appropriate to the culture?
- Has the culture contributed to effective labour performance (labour turnover or productivity)?
- Is the culture compatible with the structure of the organisation?

If there are positive answers to many of the above questions, the senior management may not be under too much pressure to change the culture of the organisation.

But there are situations in which an ability to change is important: an organisation may operate in a changing environment, it may change its structure or appoint new senior managers with different leadership styles. In such circumstances, being able to change culture could be an important part of commercial success.

Whether Paul Wagstaff is correct depends upon the nature of the business and the environment in which the firm operates. Industries in which change is rapid and the demands placed upon employees are ever changing may require firms to change culture. Other factors, such as the financial position of the business, may determine whether a company needs to change its culture.

## Discuss the view that delayering only ever has a positive impact in the long run.

**(40 marks)**

There are many arguments in favour of the viewpoint expressed in the title of the question. The need for training and the disruption and damage to morale caused by possible redundancies can mean that, in the short term, performance may suffer.

However, if preparation for delayering is effective, implementation may be smooth and it is less likely to have an adverse effect on the organisation.

You could argue that, whether this view is proved correct for any particular business may depend upon factors such as:

- the quality and experience of the managers implementing delayering
- the extent and detail of the preparation for this change
- whether employees are involved in the decision
- whether it is a cost-saving exercise or a genuine attempt to delegate authority and enrich the jobs of those on the shop floor.

# Student answers: The structure and culture of organisations

## Analyse the benefits a small business operating in a rapidly changing market might gain from having an enterprise culture.

**(9 marks)**

### Student answer

A rapidly changing market imposes a number of pressures on a business. It will require a business to make quick decisions to avoid being left behind by competitors or losing touch with their customers. An enterprise culture will assist a business in taking rapid decisions because it concentrates control in the hands of a few people.

An enterprise culture might be appropriate in these circumstances because it is possible for the manager of a small business to have a clear overview of all that is happening in the organisation. By taking this approach, the manager can avoid some of the dangers of delegation, as well as ensuring that all decisions made within the organisation help to achieve corporate objectives.

### *Marker's comments*

*This is a good quality answer. It focuses on the question throughout and has it well organised in two separate paragraphs. This format encourages analytical writing: the essence of analysis in examinations is to develop a few points fully by following through a line of argument. The structure encourages an analytical answer.*

**Mark: Content 2/2, Application 4/4, Analysis 2/3, Total = 8**

## To what extent might the style of leadership shape the structure of the organisation?

**(11 marks)**

### Student answer

The style adopted by the leader will shape the structure of the organisation. Under a democratic management style, the business is likely to be relatively flat – probably a matrix structure. This type of structure allows relatively easy two-way communication, which is an important part of democratic leadership. An organisation with many layers of hierarchy would find it difficult to communicate easily and messages could become distorted.

Democratic managers may wish to implement delegation throughout the organisation and a matrix structure would make this easier.

Similarly, an autocratic leader may be more concerned about retaining control and is likely to develop an organisation with a number of levels of hierarchy and clear definitions of jobs and responsibilities.

In evaluation, it is true to say that the style of leadership will be the most important factor in deciding the organisation's structure.

### *Marker's Comments*

*The student has only partly answered this question. He or she obviously has some relevant subject knowledge and limited mastery of the skills necessary to respond successfully to questions such as this. The major error was to address just one side of the question. The answer offered some arguments in support of the view but did not consider the other side of the case. The phrase 'To what extent ...' should trigger a two-sided answer and some genuine evaluation.*

*The evaluation was a sham. It is much easier to write evaluatively following some consideration of both sides of a particular argument. Examiners will not be fooled by the use of phrases such as 'In evaluation ...'.*

**Mark: Content 2/2, Application & Analysis 4/6, Evaluation 0/3, Total = 6**

# Examine the factors that may influence a management team when deciding upon a new structure for an organisation.

**(9 marks)**

## Student answer

A management team might be influenced by the skills that the workforce of the business possesses. If the workforce is relatively unskilled then it is more likely that a traditional and hierarchical structure will be used. This will allow supervision of employees and support in unfamiliar circumstances. A skilled workforce may operate within a matrix structure to allow the firm to gain full benefit from the employees' skills.

The nature of the product and the market in which the firm operates may be important factors. A firm producing technical products in a rapidly changing market may find traditional, hierarchical structures too inflexible in a dynamic environment. Managers may find that a matrix structure is more appropriate, allowing the business to operate project teams to develop new products and to consider ways to improve the business's position within the market.

### *Marker's comments*

*This is a solid, competent answer. It uses subject knowledge effectively and applies it consistently to the question. It makes effective use of paragraphs to highlight the extent and quality of the analysis.*

*This is a good example of how to respond to a question calling for analysis. The only slight weakness is that it loses its way a little towards the end of the second paragraph.*

**Mark: Content 2/2, Application 4/4, Analysis 2/3, Total = 8**

# Discuss the preparations that a large business should take prior to implementing a policy of decentralisation.

**(11 marks)**

## Student answer

The business needs to train the employees who are going to take on different roles following the introduction of decentralisation. This training could fall into two types:

- Training on the job – this means that employees are trained in their place of work, perhaps by more experienced colleagues. Sometimes this is referred to as 'sitting next to Nellie'. This type of training is cheaper than some others and does prepare workers directly for the job they are doing, or are about to do. It also means that the employees are not absent from their place of work for long periods of time.
- External training is the other possibility – this is perhaps more appropriate to the employees in the question. Employees in this situation will require some management training, to prepare them to take on some of the responsibilities formerly held by people in the head office.

Other ways in which the firm could prepare would include looking at communication channels and administrative systems to allow decision-making away from the top.

## *Marker's comments*

*The student has made a common error in response to this question. He or she started by making a relevant point about training, but then went on to rewrite a section of class notes before, realising the mistake, belatedly beginning to address the question.*

*It is vital to apply subject knowledge to the circumstances of the question and to ensure that your answer is relevant throughout. In spite of a few good points towards the end, this was a weak answer.*

**Mark: Content 2/2, Application & Analysis 2/6, Evaluation 0/3, Total = 4**

# *End of section questions*

1 Discuss the reasons why modern businesses pay close attention to their organisational culture.

(11 marks)

2 To what extent can the culture of a firm determine its success?

(11 marks)

3 Discuss the factors that might lead to an organisation implementing a task culture.

(11 marks)

4 Analyse the ways in which a firm's structure may influence its performance.

(9 marks)

5 H. J. Smith is a long-established and paternalistic medium-sized company. Discuss the advantages and disadvantages that may result from a decision to delayer.

(11 marks)

6 Analyse how the role of a senior manager might change as a result of a decision to flatten the organisational structure.

(9 marks)

7 Examine the benefits a multi-national manufacturer might expect as a result of a policy of decentralisation.

(9 marks)

8 To what extent is the culture of a business determined by the business's structure?

(11 marks)

9 Consider the factors that may prompt a business to attempt to change its culture.

(11 marks)

10 Analyse the difficulties a business might encounter as a result of having a strong organisational culture.

(9 marks)

# *Essays*

1 'The prime motive for businesses to restructure is to reduce the size of the corporate wage bill.' Critically assess this statement.

(40 marks)

2 The fact that some firms are decentralising at the same time as others are centralising suggests that managers cannot make up their mind as to the best way to organise their businesses. To what extent do you agree with this view?

(40 marks)

3 The manager of a major UK retailer is reported to have commented: 'It is more important for all European businesses to have a change culture rather than simply to change their culture'. Evaluate this opinion.

(40 marks)

4 'If an organisation is well led, then the structure of the organisation is of little importance.' Discuss this statement.

(40 marks)

5 The newly appointed chief executive of an unsuccessful business commented: 'There is little point in blaming the culture of the organisation for failure to meet corporate objectives. The truth is that this is frequently an excuse for weak leadership'. Evaluate this statement.

(40 marks)

CHAPTER 5

# Communication in business

## *Introduction*

Communication in modern businesses can take many forms. If asked to start a list, meetings and memos would come to mind. However, new forms of communication are revolutionising the business world. Increasingly, businesses are using electronic technology to communicate as the scale and diversity of their operations grow. Informal communication is also important as it can work both to an organisation's benefit and disadvantage. Communication in general raises important issues for managers and students of business studies. We shall address these in this chapter.

KEY TERM

**Communication** is a transportation mechanism for transferring information between people.

### Communication and motivation

Communication lies at the heart of any policy designed to motivate the workforce. The interrelationship between communication and motivation is worthy of analysis and provides increased understanding of what is arguably an organisation's greatest asset: its workforce. We shall cover this aspect also.

FACT FILE

British Telecom has led the way in using e-mail as a part of its day-to-day activities. Over 70,000 BT employees have access to e-mail and the system handles 12 million messages each month.

**Knowing what to do, getting it done correctly (and knowing it has been done correctly) relies on effective communication.**

## *Communication: the key to corporate success?*

The results of a 1998 survey by the Institute of Management and UMIST highlighted the continuing importance of communication within businesses. Interestingly, the results echoed the findings of a similar survey the previous year.

The survey reported that poor communication led to insecurity amongst junior and middle managers, as they knew little about corporate strategies. Good communication, by comparison, can help employees at all levels within the hierarchy by:

- making it easier to implement change
- developing commitment from all employees to the organisation

**KEY TERMS**

**Feedback**
is a response to communication. It may confirm the arrival of the message and indicate whether it has been understood.

**Informal communication**
takes place outside the official channels of an organisation – gossip is a prime example.

- ensuring that all areas of the organisation are pursuing the same corporate objectives.

**Communication is vital in a changing world. Arguably the most important action top managers can take to provide a better environment for employees is to improve communication within the organisation.**

The survey highlighted that, in a business world which is experiencing unprecedented rates of change, employees can quickly lose touch with what is happening. This can result in demotivated and demoralised staff and the potential to affect adversely the performance of the organisation.

## Why is communication important?

All organisations need to communicate effectively (internally and externally) if they are to survive in a competitive business environment. Effective communication offers businesses a number of benefits.

**The job of the manager is to communicate with everyone – shareholders, the media, superiors, customers and suppliers. The measure of today's managers is how well they communicate and not so much what they communicate.**

## Benefits of good communication

Good communication can have a positive impact upon employee motivation and performance. Praise and recognition are widely seen as motivators, but rely upon communication. Communication can also give employees important feedback about their performance and help them to improve it in the future. In this respect, appraisal systems have been of considerable value.

Communication is the cornerstone of co-ordination. Especially in large businesses, it is easy for different departments or parts of the organisation to pursue differing objectives. Regular and effective communication can help to ensure that all employees remain closely focused on agreed corporate objectives.

Effective communication with customers is essential for businesses. The pursuit of quality means that businesses have to satisfy customers' needs. A key element here is to establish exactly what the customer requires – perhaps through market research. It is also important to make sure that these needs are being satisfied on an ongoing basis.

Successful decision-making requires that managers have access to as much relevant information as possible. If managers are unaware of technological developments, for example, they might take a decision to purchase assets which will become obsolete within a short period of time. Good communication provides managers with the information they need, when they need it so they can make informed decisions.

Modern techniques such as just-in-time (JIT) production place great emphasis on effective communication systems. If supplies of components or raw materials are not available when required, businesses are likely to incur substantial – and unnecessary – costs. Similarly, techniques such as kaizen (continuous improvement) groups rely heavily upon effective, two-way, internal communication.

**KEY POINTS**

An organisation with effective communication is likely to have:

- a greater consistency of approach
- higher levels of motivation
- more awareness of its market and its own strengths and weakenesses
- a greater ability to respond to change effectively
- better informed decision-making.

**PROGRESS CHECK**

Analyse the ways in which better communication might improve a firm's performance.

**Information is a competitive weapon. Good communication helps firms to compete.**

## Why don't businesses improve their communication?

Surveys regularly reveal that businesses communicate badly, both internally and externally. It seems obvious that many businesses could improve performance by evaluating communication methods. There are a number of reasons to explain why businesses do not always take the necessary corrective actions.

**KEY POINTS**

Communication is an essential part of effective management. Good communication is particularly important when:

- introducing new policies and procedures
- experiencing a crisis or some period of rapid change
- undertaking reorganisations or structural change
- operating in a rapidly changing market.

### Ignorance

Many managers do not know that communication within their organisations is not effective. Symptoms of poor communication (such as poor industrial relations and low levels of motivation) may be attributed to other factors. The fact that senior managers have access to all the information they require and can communicate easily may disguise the fact that others in the business do not enjoy these privileges.

### Leadership style

Some managers use leadership styles which discourage effective two-way communication within the business. They may feel more comfortable with an autocratic leadership style and a traditional organisational structure along with downward communication.

### Size and complexity

Organisations are increasing in scale and becoming ever more complex. For example, some major multi-nationals operate across the globe, spanning dozens of cultures and possibly hundreds of languages. As a consequence, the need for information has increased dramatically but it has become more difficult to meet this demand.

**KEY TERM**

**Internal communication** takes place between individuals or groups within the organisation.

### The broadening of roles

The need for information (and thus communication) has been further increased by developments such as delegation, empowerment, decentralisation, just-in-time and

KEY TERMS

**Downward communication** describes a situation in which the predominant flow of communication in an organisation is from higher levels within the hierarchy to lower levels.

**Two-way communication** exists when information is passed up the organisational structure as well as down it.

FACT FILE

Recent research by accountants KPMG has discovered that directors of UK companies spend an average of 11% of their working lives sending and responding to e-mails.

KEY POINTS

Firms are less likely to improve their communication when:

- the managers do not realise there is a problem
- they lack the necessary resources to introduce new technology
- the existing communication is good
- the management style is authoritarian

kaizen groups. Extending the roles and authority of employees creates a greater need for information, as well as opening up new channels of communication. The use of core and peripheral employees, consultants and contract workers has further complicated the picture.

## Information technology (IT)

Many observers believe that IT can solve the communications problems that many businesses face. They cite the benefits provided by databases, e-mail, Intranets and the Internet in support of their case. On the contrary, some firms have found that IT, by virtue of the amount of data it can generate, adds to the communication problems faced by many businesses. Managers are overwhelmed by information and cannot decide which of it is important. We shall consider IT and communication more fully later in this chapter.

Of course, communication is important in all businesses. Many managers would argue that it is *the key* to successful management (and those who do not probably do not appreciate its importance!). However, improving communication does not always cure a business's problems. Other factors such as the quality of product and customer service, the extent of the product range, the skills and enthusiasm of the workforce and the utilisation of assets will all play important parts in determining the competitiveness of a business. Nevertheless, the key management roles of **planning**, **prioritising**, **co-ordinating** and **controlling** depend on *access to information.*

PROGRESS CHECK

## Questions

1 You have 5 minutes to convince a busy chief executive that she should spend a large sum of money improving communications within her business, rather than purchasing new manufacturing equipment. Outline the arguments you would use.
2 Why might managers of large businesses be particularly slow to improve communications within their organisations?
3 Discuss the possible reasons why organisations fail to improve their communications.

PROGRESS CHECK

Many managers know that communication in their organisations is poor. Analyse the possible reasons why it is not improved.

# *Communication and technology*

It is relatively simple to list the new forms of communication that have arisen as a result of improvements in technology. Business magazines are full of articles on how to use the worldwide web to improve communications with customers and how e-mail can revolutionise a firm's internal communication. Developments such as fax machines, e-mails, the Internet and Intranets all make it easier to send and receive messages and, generally, improve the flow of information. It would seem, therefore, that technology can help to solve the age-old problem of poor communication, whilst enhancing the performance of employees and businesses alike.

KEY TERMS

**Internet**
links computers across the world allowing communication and commercial activity between an estimated 50 million users.

**Intranets**
link computers within an individual business allowing employees to use e-mail and access to a range of on-line services.

## How can IT improve performance?

Visionaries see the future of business changing radically because of developments in communications technology. These developments will, we are assured, result in happier and better motivated employees and more efficient and profitable businesses. Technology will enable the 'mobile' worker to carry out his or her duties at home or in the car; visits to the office will be infrequent. In the United States about 10% of workers are mobile and the trend is apparent in other countries, notably Norway, Sweden and Denmark. Some firms have reported a reduction in office space of up to 50% as a result of switching employees to a mobile basis. This has cut overheads dramatically.

### Automation

Communications technology has also offered businesses the opportunity to replace people with technology. Automatic telephone answering systems and voicemail have, for example, reduced the need for receptionists, whilst managers communicating through e-mail have cut the number of secretaries required. Reductions in the wage bill have helped businesses to control costs and remain competitive.

FACT FILE

**BT/Cellnet is set to update office communications by launching its corporate One-Phone. This acts as a cordless (but normal) 'phone within the office, and switches to a mobile outside the building. A major benefit of this development is that it would remove the need for separate telephone numbers.**

### Management Information Systems

An effective and efficient **Management Information System** (MIS) can provide managers with an accurate and up-to-date picture of what is happening in the business. It can provide data on stocks, staff, orders, budgets, costs and revenues as well as forecasting and drafting financial statements. A modern MIS relies on computer technology but has the potential to provide first-class data and improve decision-making.

### Technology in marketing

Other benefits from communications technology for businesses relate to marketing. The Internet allows even relatively small firms to sell their products throughout the World, without the need for agents or retail outlets. A combination of a well-designed website and the ability to purchase by credit card can permit a small US business, for example, to sell its wares throughout Europe. The market potential is certain to grow as more consumers link up to the worldwide web. Many UK businesses have developed attractive and informative websites as part of their corporate marketing strategy and, increasingly, website addresses are appearing in traditional forms of advertising.

KEY TERM

A **Management Information System** is a mechanism, usually computer-based, which is designed to provide managers with the information they require at the time it is needed.

### Technology in production

Communications technology has also been behind a revolution in the production processes used by many businesses. Sophisticated just-in-time manufacturing systems offer firms the benefits of holding minimal stocks; they rely upon information technology for automatic ordering of replacement stock and components, in line with future patterns of demand. **Extranets**, which link computers in different firms, service JIT production and other information needs. Sensitive 'pull' systems of production could not operate without modern IT.

FACT FILE

An American company has designed what they claim to be the World's most powerful computer. Silicon Graphics claim that their Blue Mountain computer cost £73 million to develop and is 15,000 times faster than a personal computer.

KEY TERM

**An Extranet** links the computers of one business to those of its suppliers and retailers, allowing the effective exchange of information between key commercial partners.

## Technology in people management

Communications technology has supported many of the developments in managing and organising employees that have occurred over recent years. As we have seen, many changes in business have given managers broader spans of control and mean that they have to make extensive use of delegation to keep their workloads under control. Such management techniques require subordinates to communicate regularly with their managers and colleagues. Using technology in the form of faxes, voicemail, e-mail and Intranets has facilitated this process and contributed to development and implementation of modern methods of production and people management.

PROGRESS CHECK

**Examine the ways in which developments in communications technology can improve a firm's performance.**

FACT FILE

Bass, the Midland brewer, operates an Intranet recording details of suppliers. Bass employees are only able to place orders with companies whose details appear on their internal computer system.

FACT FILE

In the late 1990s, Cable and Wireless Communications agreed a £1.8 billion contract with IBM to manage its computer systems over a 10 year period. As a consequence of the deal 950 Cable and Wireless staff transferred to IBM.

# Problems with communications technology

Technology does not always provide the cure for inadequate communication that many managers have hoped for. It has the potential to improve the flow of information within the organisation but it can bring a number of associated problems:

- *Cost* – communications technology is expensive and, because of the rapid pace of technological change, it is likely to need replacing frequently. An ongoing commitment to modern forms of communication can prove to be a major drain on an organisation's financial resources. Investing in the latest IT equipment may mean that the business is unable to purchase other vital assets, for example new production equipment.
- *Research and planning* are essential if Information Technology is to have a positive impact upon communication within the business.
- *Expectations* – managers need to determine exactly what they expect to gain from new technology before installing it. One major newspaper withdrew its voicemail system only days after it was installed because the editor feared that someone calling in with a scoop might not bother to speak to a machine.
- *Training* is important to ensure employees understand how the system works and how to get the best out of it.
- *Customer service* – some evidence exists to support the view that communications technology is highly unpopular with customers. A survey by BT showed that 70% of callers hang up without saying anything when confronted by a